KENTUCKY'S GERMAN PIONEERS

H. A. Rattermann's History

Translated and Edited by
Don Heinrich Tolzmann

HERITAGE BOOKS
2007

HERITAGE BOOKS

AN IMPRINT OF HERITAGE BOOKS, INC.

Books, CDs, and more—Worldwide

For our listing of thousands of titles see our website
at
www.HeritageBooks.com

Published 2007 by
HERITAGE BOOKS, INC.
Publishing Division
65 East Main Street
Westminster, Maryland 21157-5026

International Standard Book Number: 978-0-7884-1735-1

Table of Contents

Editor's Preface

This work consists of a collection of articles translated from German, which originally appeared in the well-known 19th century German-American historical journal, *Der Deutsche Pionier*, published in Cincinnati by the German Pioneer Society, and which was edited for the greater part of its existence by H.A. Rattermann. Although it's focus was primarily on the Greater Cincinnati area, it also covered German-American history in general, and the Ohio Valley in particular. Due to these interests, it contained a number of articles dealing with Kentucky, and a series of them by Rattermann dealt with German immigration and settlement in the 18th and early 19th centuries. Given the absence of a history of the Kentucky Germans, I decided to translate and edit these articles together as a contribution to an understanding of the role German-Americans have played in the history of the state of Kentucky. As approximately one-fourth of Kentuckians claim German ancestry, it is obvious that they form one of the major ethnic components in the state, and that the history of Kentucky is incomplete without their story being told. This work, therefore, provides access to some basic source materials and information on the Kentucky Germans from the beginnings to the mid-19th century, and will hopefully also provide the point of departure for all future work on the history of the Kentucky Germans.

Don Heinrich Tolzmann

Editor's Foreword

Kentucky is probably not usually thought of as a German heritage state. However, already by 1790 the state's population was 14% German, and by the time of the 1990 U.S. Census, the population of German ancestry had risen to 22%, thereby making the German element a major ethnic component in the state. By way of comparison, Louisiana is well known for its French heritage, as 23% of the state is of French descent. Considering that Kentucky is as German as Louisiana is French, the question arises as to whether the general view of Kentucky is in need of revision, as Kentucky has a great deal more German heritage than is generally known.

Given its location in the heart of the Ohio Valley, where one finds states adjacent to it with substantial populations of German heritage, Kentucky's percentage of German heritage is not altogether surprising. In West Virginia and Virginia to the east the German element is 26.2% and 19.24 respectively; to the north in Ohio, Indiana, and Illinois it is 37.5%, 37.6%, and 29.1%; to the west Missouri it is 36%; and even Tennessee to the south has a German element of 14.9%.[1]

Although one finds brief, scattered references to German immigration and settlement, there has been no general history of the topic available, and the public awareness of Kentucky's German element is negligible. According to Thomas P. Baldwin, "many Kentuckians are probably unaware that Germans and those of German descent were among the early explorers and settlers in Kentucky...Both the Kentucky rifle and the Conestoga wagon originated in the German areas of Pennsylvania, and the Appalachian dulcimer is of German origin."[2]

There are several reasons why so little is known of Kentucky's German heritage. Perhaps the foremost factor has to do with the stereotype about Kentucky, and what a Kentuckian is. John Leighly notes that "the usual conception of the pioneer population of Kentucky does not include recognition of a noteworthy German element; popular lore and both scholarly and popular literature have established the stereotype of the Appalachian Anglo-Saxon retaining traces of Elizabethan speech, with a possible admixture of Scotch-Irish."[3]

The publications of Kentucky presses by and large continue to perpetuate this popular stereotype, and have completely overlooked the German heritage of the state. The stereotype about Kentuckians as being

Appalachians of Anglo stock unfortunately obscures the diversity of the state in general, and the role of the German element in particular.

A second factor to take into consideration is that German settlers of the 18th and 19th century early on became an integral part of the very fabric of the state, and may be said to have contributed greatly to it as a co-founding element. German-Americans and their contributions came, therefore, to be seen as merely a part of the socio-cultural landscape of Kentucky, and were taken for granted, which has also generally been the case elsewhere in the U.S. when it comes to a history of German-Americans.

A third factor, is that references to German-Americans in state and local histories are few and far between, and most do not even refer to them as such. Before 1848, when ethnic heritage was mentioned, Germans were often referred to as "Dutch," as Germans were known at the time. When German-American names appear they are often Anglicized, or even translated. For example, the name Steiner often became Stoner, and the name Zimmermann was translated as Carpenter. Hence, when such names are mentioned, it requires close examination to ascertain if they are German, or not.

A fourth factor was that of the anti-German hysteria and sentiment of the world wars. It was especially during the First World War that a considerable amount of German-Americana was lost, as libraries burned, destroyed or trashed their holdings of books, newspapers, and other publications in the German language. Although a total of 48 German-language newspapers appeared in Kentucky, they have all but completely vanished, save for a few.

Indeed, it is remarkable that in cities and towns where German newspapers were printed, and which would have contained valuable historical information on the area, that not a trace of these publications can be found. Only since the celebration of the American Bicentennial in 1976, has the field of German-American Studies flourished, and continued the work of telling the story of the German-American experience. However, the task is rendered all that more difficult by the loss of source materials.

This work aims to tell the story of the German immigration and settlement of Kentucky approximately to the date of 1848, or the time of the 1848 Revolution in Europe, which marks a new period in German-American history with the arrival of the so-called Forty-Eighters and the massive waves of immigration in the 1850s.

The period up to 1848 may, therefore, be regarded as the first and foundational period in the history of Kentucky's German element, when German immigration and settlement began. As this work shows, Germans concentrated in this period, almost exclusively in the Blue Grass Region. For this reason, this work focuses on that area. This is not to say that Germans did not settle elsewhere in Kentucky, but that they were mainly concentrated in this area of the state.

The purpose of this work is to provide an introduction to Kentucky's German heritage by means of a survey of the history of German immigration and settlement in Kentucky, from the beginnings and up to 1848. To accomplish this task, I have translated and edited a series of articles by Heinrich A. Rattermann, the well known German-American historian, who edited an historical journal, *Der Deutsche Pionier*, in Cincinnati, Ohio. Although I had originally planned on writing a history of the Kentucky Germans, it seemed to me that Rattermann's articles contained such a wealth of information and detail that this kind of primary source material was worthy of being made available in translation. What is of special value is that Rattermann searched through county and local records, seeking out evidence of the early German pioneers. It is especially valuable for recording the influx of German-American veterans of the American Revolution into Kentucky. Rattermann also attempts to provide a picture of life in early Kentucky as experienced by the Kentucky German pioneers. This collection, therefore, provides access to the early history of the Kentucky Germans, and is in and of itself an important historical document in the history of Kentucky. Unfortunately, Rattermann never completed his work, and articles on Louisville and Covington were not published.

To supplement and complement the work I have, therefore, added an article by another German-American historian, Gustav Koerner, dealing with the Louisville Germans, which cover the period up to about 1848. In addition, I have also added a brief chapter on the topic of Covington, Kentucky to provide complete coverage of the Blue Grass Region for the period under consideration. This work, hence, concentrates on the pre-1848, or pioneer period of Kentucky's German heritage.[4] Footnotes by Rattermann are indicated by the initials "HAR," and those of the editor as by "DHT."

Notes

1. For a listing of population statistics by state, see Gerard Wilk, *Americans From Germany*, Edited by Don Heinrich Tolzmann. (Indianapolis: Max Kade German-American Center, Indiana University-Purdue University & Indiana German Heritage Society, 1995), p. 83.

2. Thomas P. Baldwin, "German Settlement," in: John E. Kleber, ed., *The Kentucky Encyclopedia*. (Lexington: University Press of Kentucky, 1992), 372. Although close to one-fourth of the state's population, this is the only survey of Kentucky's German heritage that is available in English.

3. John Leighly, *German Family Names in Kentucky Place Names*. (New York: American Name Society, 1983), p. 6. Kentucky is a state defined by several geographical regions: the Eastern Coal Field in the east, the Blue Grass Region in central and northern Kentucky, the Pennroyal Region in the southwestern part of the state, the Western Coal Field, in the northwest, and far to the west, the Jackson Purchase. If any one section is readily identifiable with the stereotype that Leighly describes is really the Eastern Coal Field, and not the entire state by any means. As noted, the German element concentrated early on in central and northern Kentucky in what became known as the Blue Grass Region.

4. Rattermann's articles appeared in: *Der Deutsche Pionier*. 9(1877): 84-94, 258-64, 309-15, 352-57; 10(1878): 272-78, 368-73; 11(1879): 65-72, 181-84, 425-31; 12(1880): 65-73, 93-99, 136-43, 298-305, 444-50. For biographical information on Rattermann, see Don Heinrich Tolzmann, ed., *German-American Literature*. (Metuchen, New Jersey: Scarecrow Press, 1977), pp. 240-44. The chapter on Louisville is from: Gustav Koerner, *Das deutsche Element in den Vereinigten Staaten von Nordamerika, 1818-1848*. (Cincinnati: A.E. Wilde & Co., 1880).

Editor's Introduction

Kentucky

Prior to the French and Indian War (1754-63), the territory located west of the Appalachian Mountains and east of the Mississippi was the focal point of international politics, and was claimed and contested by both France and England. Kentucky itself was located in the heart of the Ohio River Valley, which consisted of the Ohio River and its tributaries and adjoining land. This included: West Virginia, Western Pennsylvania, Ohio, Indiana, Illinois, Tennessee, and, of course, Kentucky, which swiftly filled up with settlers after the French and Indian War, won by Great Britain. After the American Revolution, settlers streamed into Kentucky, so that in 1792, Kentucky entered the Union as the 14th state, at which time it had a population of 74,000 settlers.[1]

European Exploration

The European discovery of the Ohio River Valley dates to 1673, when the French trader, Louis Jolliet, and Father Jacque Marquette came upon the Ohio River, where it meets with the great Mississippi. However, they did not explore it, but proceeded south on the Mississippi. The French explorer LaSalle, conducted an expedition in 1681-82 on the Mississippi as a part of the French attempt to dominate the fur trade of the west, and traversed the Ohio Valley region. In 1692-94, Arnout Viele, a Dutch trader and Indian interpreter, who worked for the English, traveled from Albany, New York down the Ohio River well past the present day city of Cincinnati, and perhaps not far from today's Louisville, for the purpose of trading with the Shawnees. These early adventurers appear to have been the first European attempts to explore the Ohio River Valley.

At roughly the same time explorers were beginning to look westward from the east. In 1670, Johann Lederer, a young German doctor made three trips, but did not climb the eastern slopes of the Blue Ridge Mountains. Thereafter, others ventured west as well, and by 1699, the Virginians had gained enough knowledge of the land across the Appalachian Mountains to realize how close they actually were to the French, who in that year established their first settlements in Louisiana.

In 1727, the French surveyed the Allegheny and upper Ohio rivers, and in 1730 established posts at Fort Vincennes, Fort Oniatenon, and Fort Miami in Indiana. In 1751-52, the Ohio Valley opened up to English traders as a result of the treaties negotiated with the Six Nations of the Iroquois Federation, and with the Miami, Shawnee, and Delaware tribes. The French response was the destruction of a trading post on the Miami River belonging to George Croghan, who had negotiated the treaties with the assistance of the German frontiersman, Conrad Weiser.

This was followed by the building of forts by the French to stave of the advance of the English. At one of them, Fort Duquesne, the Virginia militia under George Washington battled the French, beginning the conflict between the French and the English, which ultimately led to the defeat of the French in 1760 that resulted in the Treaty of Paris (1763). This so-called French and Indian War stated that North America east of the Mississippi was now in the possession of Great Britain, which opened up the entire region to settlement.

By the 1740s, Indian traders and frontiersmen were heading west over the Appalachians, and were being joined by land speculators, as well as land companies. In 1750, Dr Thomas Walker, a physician and explorer, led an expedition that discovered a pass through the mountains that became known as the Cumberland Gap, which played a major role in the opening up of the region, and became a major passage way for settlers moving west. In 1751, Christopher Gist of Maryland reached the lowlands of eastern Kentucky as an agent of the Ohio Company as a further indication of interest in the area.

The British Proclamation of 1763 stated that settlements west of the Appalachians were banned, but colonists from Pennsylvania, Virginia, and the Carolinas continued westward, making use of military roads cut by the British during the French and Indian War. Most alluring of all were the hills and blue grass of Kentucky. In 1766, several parties passed through the Cumberland Gap, and news of their travels reached and attracted Daniel Boone, who made his first trip to Kentucky in 1767-68.

With John Finley as his guide, Boone reached the Gap in 1769, and proceeded into eastern Kentucky. By 1774, there was a settlement at Harrodsburg, but the Shawnee tried desperately to stamp out further western advancements. However, after their defeat, western settlement was secured, and Britain helped clear the way by means of the building of the Wilderness

Road. By 1776, the frontier had been pushed back, and in less than two decades Kentucky would become a state.

German Immigration and Settlement

The first Germans to settle in what became the United States, arrived at the English settlement at Jamestown, Virginia on 1 October 1608, and on 6 October 1683, the first permanent all-German settlement at Germantown, Pennsylvania.[2] By the time of the American Revolution in 1776, about 10% of the total population of 2.5 millions in the colonies were of German stock. Although found in all colonies, half of the colonial German element was concentrated in one colony, Pennsylvania. Germans were also particularly concentrated in New York, Virginia and Maryland.

Frederick Jackson Turner noted in his *The Frontier in American History* that by the time of the American Revolution "a zone of almost continuous German settlement had been established, running from the head of the Mohawk in New York to Savannah, Georgia."[3]

German immigration and settlement in Kentucky in the 18th and early 19th century can be placed in the broader context of the European interest and exploration of the west, followed later by that of the U.S., and can be seen as part of the western movement of German settlers on the American frontier.

The first German settlers came primarily from the Carolinas, Virginia, and Pennsylvania. Their main route was via the Cumberland Gap, and their settlement area of choice was the Blue Grass Region of Kentucky. In the course of 19th century more settlers came from these regions to Kentucky, but increasingly they came by means of the Ohio River.

By the 1830s, direct immigration from Europe was arriving, and tended to concentrate in the river cities, towns, and settlements along the Ohio River, but remaining within the older settlement area of the Blue Grass Region. Although they would settle elsewhere in the state, this region remained their major area of settlement, and here the urban centers of German-American life and culture would thrive.

The history of Kentucky's German heritage is one that needs to be told, and this work is a contribution to an understanding of German immigration and settlement in the Blue Grass state that reaches back to the 18th century.

Notes

1. For a basic handbook of Kentucky history, see John E. Kleber, ed., *The Kentucky Encyclopedia*. (Lexington: University Press of Kentucky, 1992).

2. See Don Heinrich Tolzmann, ed., *The First Germans in America, With a Biographical Directory of New York Germans*. (Bowie, MD: Heritage Books, Inc., 1992).

3. Cited in: Don Heinrich Tolzmann, ed., *Wisconsin's German Element: J.H. A. Lacher's Introductory History*. (Baltimore: Clearfield Press, 1999), p. 5.

I. The 18th and Early 19th Centuries

1. The German Pioneers

Nowhere else, with the exception of Pennsylvania, Texas, and Wisconsin, was the settlement of a region by Germans so important as in Kentucky, and nowhere else has their role been so forgotten.[1] The number of German hunters and settlers, who came to Kentucky in the 18th and early 19th centuries, is substantial and a number of the most important pioneers of the state bear German surnames, including: Georg Jäger, Michael Steiner (Stoner), Johannes Hermann, Johannes Hagen, Joseph and Jakob Sadowsky, Peter Nieswanger, Wilhelm Christian, Michael Schuck, Leonard Helm, and countless others.[2]

And wasn't it even claimed that the pioneer of all pioneers, Daniel Boone, was German? It is common knowledge that he spoke German. The assertion, especially by Anglo-American authors, that he was of English descent, is usually advanced, but without any evidence, or reference to the names of the parents.[3] We, however, certainly don't make any such claims that Boone was a German, or of German stock, as there are more than enough German names among the pioneers, which show what an important element German stock was with the pioneers of early Kentucky, and we shall, therefore, try to tell their story.

Early in July 1773 a party of backwoodsmen with several land surveyors, led by the surveyor Robert McAfee, proceeded from Botetourte County, Virginia to the recently discovered western paradise, which was then called "Kain-tuck-ee," to take possession of what land they could. While the surveyors did their job on the lower Salt Lick River, Captain Jacob Harrod and 31 others arrived early in the new year coming down the Ohio River on a flatboat.

They traveled up the Kentucky River, and founded the first white settlement in Kentucky in what is today Mercer County. This was named Harrodstown for its founder, later Oldtown, and today Harrodsburg.

Who all belonged to this party, cannot exactly be determined. However, we know that there was a German member: Johannes Hermann. In 1774, he planted and harvested the first corn in Kentucky. This cornfield war located in the eastern end of town.[4] Other German members of this party were: Abraham Heit (Hite), the brothers Joseph and Jakob Sadowsky and Captain Abraham Schöplein (Chapline), the latter of whom discovered a branch of the Salt River, which was then named for him as "Chapline River."[5]

The little town was divided up into half-acre building lots with five acre outlots. Several log houses were then built, which they moved into in June, thus beginning the oldest settlement of Kentucky. Shortly thereafter, on 20 July, four settlers discovered a magnificent spring about three miles downstream, which they named Fountainbleau due to its wonderful location. They then camped there for a midday rest, when they were suddenly surprised by Indians, who fired on them and killed one of their party, Jared Cowen, whereupon they all fled.

Jakob Sadowsky and another member of the party then jumped into a canoe at the river bank, and as they were then cut off by the Indians from returning to the settlement, they headed downstream to the Ohio River, from whence they traveled farther all the way to New Orleans. From here they sailed to Philadelphia, and then to Virginia. The fourth member of the group made his way back to the camp by means of a number of detours. He informed the settlement of Indians. Captain Harrod and several of his armed associates then made their way to the site and buried Cowen, but nothing was seen of the Indians.[6]

In the fall, they were visited by Daniel Boone who together with Michael Steiner had been dispatched by Governor Dunmore to bring news to the surveyors at the Ohio falls regarding the uprising of the Indians, which had led to the battle at the mouth of the Kanawha, which General Lewis had fought on 10 October 1774. On receiving this news, all the settlers left the area to return to the settlements near the Clinch River, so that they could winter there. In the following spring the McAfee party again proceeded to the Salt Lick River to continue surveying the area. A few days later, Captain Harrod and his people passed through on their way to Harrodsburg.

After returning to Virginia, the McAffee party sent two of its group (John Higgins and Edwin Paulsen) on 11 April to guard their land.[7] At the same time, another party came from North Carolina with the intention of settling in Kentucky. Col. Richard Henderson and several other speculators had acquired two sizable pieces of land from the Cherokees, apparently for the amount of 10,000 Pounds Sterling. This was after the peace, which Lord Dunmore had established with the Indians in November 1774 at Camp Charlotte, in what is today Pickaway County, Ohio.

These land acquisitions consisted of, first: the entire east Tennessee region at the Holstein (now: Holsten) River, from the border of North

Carolina to the Cumberland River, and, second: all land between the Cumberland and the Kentucky Rivers, with the Ohio River as the northern boundary.

What right the Cherokees possessed with regard to the latter of the two, can not be determined here, as Kentucky was viewed generally as neutral territory and common hunting ground by the six nations of the Iroquois Confederation, which resided north of the Ohio River and by the Cherokees and other Indians, who lived south of the Cumberland Mountains.[3]

These Indian people did their hunting in Kentucky, which was also the site of warfare as well. As a result of the battles between the northern and southern Indians the land received the name "Kain-tuck-ee," the dark and bloody ground. Lord Dunmore, as Governor of Virginia, immediately raised his first protest again the acquisition of the Transylvania Company, as the company of Henderson and associates was called, and declared in a proclamation that the claims of anyone who acquired title to land from the Company was null and void.

However, this did not frighten off the North Carolinians, and so after the Treaty of Watauga (17 March 1775) a contract was concluded with Boone and others to construct a road from the settlements at the Holstein River to the Kentucky River. Boone and his associates, among them his friend and former schoolmate Michael Steiner, carried out this highly dangerous work, which required in-depth knowledge of the land, as well as wilderness road construction.[9]

The task was extremely difficult, as the land was mountainous and covered with thick bush and woods. Also, they suffered attacks by the Indians, who killed four of the workers and wounded five. The survivors completed the work and reached Kentucky in April. They immediately began work on building a fort in the vicinity of a salt spring, where Boonesborough is located today.[10]

Later, Boone brought his family here, and his wife and daughters were the first white women to have seen the banks of the Kentucky River. Thereafter, the immigration from North Carolina began to increase.[11]

In the same year two parties of hunters and squatters came to the north side of the Kentucky River, into the so-called Blue Grass region, partly with the intention of hunting, as well as to seek land for the purpose of a settlement. The first of the two was the so-called McConnell party.

Several Germans belonged to it, including: Michael Steiner, Johannes Hagen (Haggin), Jakob Dunkin, Robert Schenklein (Shanklin), and others whose names have not been preserved. In the following April (1776), this party was joined by the second, which consisted of Col. Robert Patterson, one of the founders of the three cities: Lexington, Cincinnati and Dayton; John McLelland, John Williams and the famous Indian fighter and western pioneer, Simon Kenton. They came after having built a log house for McClelland's family at Royal Springs, now Georgetown, Kentucky.[12]

The first of the two parties had come from Boonesborough to Harrodsburg for the purpose of examining the land at the Elkhorn River, and had crossed the Kentucky River in a northeast direction. There they came upon the site of the present city of Lexington, which was located by a fresh cold spring, and found the remains of a former site of the mound builders, the metropolis of a bygone race, of which there is no trace as to their name, language, or customs.

This was at the beginning of the month of June 1775, and tired from the journey, the camped out near the spring on buffalo hides, and started a fire with some dry brushwood they had gathered, and then began a frugal dinner of the ever present beef jerky. In order that they would not be surprised by an Indian attack, they placed one of the party on guard duty.

While the party was consuming its simple meal, they spoke with enthusiasm of the beautiful country they had passed through, and especially of the wonderful region where they were camped. Not surprisingly, they wanted to establish a settlement her, as the soil was the richest and most fruitful they had ever seen.

Never before had they seen such a bounty of blue grass and such rich land, as here. Deer, elk, bear, and buffalo filled the woods and meadows with game. The presence of Indians lying in wait was forgotten, as were the dangers, which would face the first settlers. With the glowing imagination that only hunters possess, they viewed the virgin splendor of the hunting grounds, which were also the ones most treasured by the Indians, and fantasized on the possibility of realizing the wonderful legends they had heard of such, such as of a distant El Dorado.[13]

William McConnell immediately began to build a simple log house, and was assisted by the other hunters. This was necessary so as to acquire the title to the land, as the state of Virginia in 1774 had declared that each settler who would clear land, build a cabin and harvest corn, would be granted the title to 400 acres of land. This was known as settler's rights at that time.[14]

In the meantime, part of the group was busy with the preliminary work for a new settlement, while the other part of the group searched the woods and thickets for game, which they found in great supply. Deer and buffalo provided their shaggy furs to the skilled huntsmen, and does and turkeys yielded a tasty feast for them.

Evenings they camped in a circle around a fire and discussed the possible names for the settlement. Patterson, who came from Yorkshire, suggested York, while Steiner and Hagen suggested Lancaster in honor of their home in Pennsylvania. However, they could not agree, perhaps because other names were suggested by the others as well.

Then an important event in the history of the country took place, that brought their discussions to an end - the Battle of Lexington. News came to them, that on 19 April, King George's troops had called the Americans rebels and had fired on them at Lexington, Massachusetts. With a cheer of "Hurrah for Lexington," they dropped all of the suggested names. This clearly demonstrated the patriotism of the hunters, who had been well weathered by the trials and tribulations of frontier life.

Lexington would be the name of the new settlement in commemoration of the day from which the seed of American freedom had blossomed.[15] "The history of the baptism of Lexington is as romantic" wrote Ranck "as the legend of the beautiful princess Pocahontas, and is more interesting because it is a based in a more actual event than the fabled legend of the founding of ancient Rome." What remarkable news from the camp of these pioneers!

At this time, when Kentucky was still an impenetrable wilderness. In the desolate stillness of night, far from all civilization, a small group of adventurers built the first monument to the first casualties of the American Revolution as a fitting and lasting tribute! Even if the ceremony was devoid of all the pomp and circumstance of fashionable society in the east or in Europe, and even if they were not attired in elegant dress, but rather in frontier clothing, bearskins and homemade fabrics and the only field music they had was the howling of the panthers and the wolves and the nocturnal hoot of the owls and the distant cry of the Indians, nevertheless this was clearly a noble act on their part, because it was inspired by the truest patriotism which can reside within the human breast.

And Mother Nature graced them with a blessing gaze in this rich and beautiful paradise. These pioneers have long since departed, but many of their graves may still be seen in the vicinity of the place, where they camped on that memorable night.

Notes

1. Rattermann here expresses concern that the role played by Germans in the settlement of Kentucky has not been adequately reflected in the standard histories of the state, and his remarks might be considered as being as valid today, as they were a century ago. The only up-to-date history of German-Americans within Kentucky is for the northern Kentucky city of Covington. See Don Heinrich Tolzmann, *Covington's German Heritage*. (Bowie, MD: Heritage Books, Inc., 1998). DHT.

2. Regarding the Virginia Germans among the pioneers of Kentucky, see Hermann Shuricht, *The German Element in Virginia*. Edited by Don Heinrich Tolzmann. (Bowie, MD: Heritage Books, Inc, 1993), Vol. 1, pp. 154-60. DHT.

3. Daniel Boone was born 11 February 1735 in Bucks County, Pa. According to American sources, he was of English descent, which was often questioned, because Bucks County was predominantly German. Also, Boone's parents in 1738 moved to the almost entirely German area of Berks County, where Daniel attended school, however only for a winter, as his parents then settled in the early 1740s in the Yadkin River area of North Carolina. Another point to consider is that Daniel spoke Pennsylvania-German as fluently as English.

He was also often held to be a German, and his name, which some felt may have evolved from Bohne to Boone, was also a question. - "His pupilage among the Germans in 'Berks County' enabled him to acquire their patois language; and it was from the circumstance of his being able to speak 'Pennsylvania German' that he was supposed to be a Dutchman, or of German extraction." J.R. Albach, *Annals of the West*. (Pittsburgh 1857), p. 212. Another example can be offered by the following: The family of Andreas Bohny arrived in Philadelphia from Rotterdam on 15 September 1729 on the ship *Allen*. (Rupp's collection of names, p. 60). The descendants of this family wrote their name later as "Boone," as is recorded in the Pennsylvania marriage registers (*Pennsylvania Archives*, 2nd Series, Vol. II, p. 36), where the marriage of Andreas Boone and Martha Gurion on 13 April 1763 is listed. HAR.

Note that Rattermann does not support the contentions that Boone was of German descent, but merely indicates that the misunderstanding was common due to the aforementioned factors. Boone's family definitely was of English origin, and arrived in America in 1717. See the editor's discussion of German influences on the Boone family, Don Heinrich Tolzmann, ed., *Abraham Lincoln's Ancestry: German or English? M.D. Learned's Investigatory History, With an Appendix on Daniel Boone.* (Bowie, MD: Heritage Books, Inc, 1993). DHT.

4. Collins, *History of Kentucky.* New Edition. (Covington, Ky, 1874), Vol. II, p. 605. - Butler, in his history of Kentucky, places this erroneously to the year 1775. Also he writes the name Hermann as Harmon. See Mann Butler *A History of the Commonwealth of Kentucky.* 2nd Edition. (Cincinnati, 1836), p. 28. Klauprecht and after him L. Stierlin write the name as Herrmann. HAR.

5. Collins. HAR.

6. Collins writes the name as "Swein Poulsen," Vol. II, p. 606. HAR.

7. They "are called by the French writers Iroquois, by the English the Five Nations and by the Indians to the southward, with whom they were at war, Massawomacs." - Jefferson, *Notes on the State of Virginia.* 8th American Edition, Appendix, p. 308. HAR.

8. John Bakeless writes of Steiner/Stoner that Boone's lifelong friend, "a large strong Dutchman, was one of the numerous Pennsylvania Germans who had migrated with others Pennsylvanians. He was a good woodsman, and so muscular that legend said when he sat down to carve his name on a tree, he often did not bother to remove the pack, weighing two or three hundred pounds, from his shoulders." See John Bakeless, *Master of the Wilderness: Daniel Boone.* (New York: William Morrow & Co., 1939), p. 77. DHT.

9. Flint, *Life of Daniel Boone.* New Edition, p. 83. HAR.

10. Regarding the Germans in North Carolina, see J.A. Wagener, "Die Deutschen in Nord-Carolina," *Der Deutsche Pionier*. 3(1871): 328-33; 4(1872): 42-45, 91-95; and also Emil Mannhardt, "Die deutsche Einwanderung in Nord-Carolina," *Deutsch-Amerikanische Geschichtsblätter*. 5:1(1905): 2-17. DHT.

11. *American Pioneer*, Vol. II, p. 344. HAR.

12. Thomas E. Pickett, in his publication "Testimony of the Mounds," p. 13, asks the question as to whether water represented a sacred element in the cult of the mound builders, as the mounds were usually located near a river and in the vicinity of a spring. HAR.

13. Geo. W. Ranck, *History of Lexington, Ky.*, p. 19. HAR.

14. Gilbert Imlay, *A Topographical Description of the Western Territory of North America*. 3rd Edition, p. 6. HAR.

15. *Bradford's Notes, Ms.* - Ranck, p. 19. HAR.

2. The Early Settlers

In late fall 1775, the backwoodsmen returned to the settlements on the other side of the mountains, but with the intention of returning in the spring and establishing a permanent settlement wherever that would be possible. The Revolutionary War, however, managed to draw the attention of the entire country into an entirely different direction, and as Kentucky was swarming with Indians who had allied themselves with the English after the outbreak of war, and who were harassing settlers on the frontier, it was, therefore, not surprising that no one thought about the loghouse of McClelland, which had contributed to the naming of a western settlement in such a romantic way.

To be sure, the province of Virginia had established the County of Kentucky on 7 December 1776 out of the gigantic wilderness of the western party of Fincastle County, but the state itself could not provide any effective defense for the settlers in the newly established county, as the war with England was claiming all the forces that could be raised. The handful of courageous pioneers in the new county had to deal, therefore, on their own terms with the Indians, who all too often were paying unwelcome visits to the widely scattered loghouses.

In the summer 1775, two daughters of Col. Calloway and one daughter of Boone were kidnaped by Fort Boonesborough by the Indians.[1] Several of the smaller stations had to be closed, including the settlement at Hinkston's Station, whose inhabitants sought refuge at McClelland's Fort, which is today Georgetown.[2]

So dangerous were the hostilities of the Indians for the settlers that at the end of the year 1776 only three settlements remained in Kentucky: Boonesborough, Harrodsburg, and St. Asaph's, or Logan's Fort, and these were held in siege in the spring of 1777 by the Indians, although without success.[3]

The western Indian tribes had been joined by the Shawnee, who previously had been friendly with the settlers.[4] Dark days, therefore, had arrived for the inhabitants of Kentucky, and still worse ones seemed to be in store for them, and many, even some of the most courageous settlers, left the land forever.[5] There remained only 102 men as the entire military force in the young settlement of Kentucky. What it had to deal with in terms of dangers, is best described by Col. J. Floyd in a letter to Col. Wm. Preston as follows:

"One sees the Indians when they lay siege to a post, rarely in full strength at a given place, but rather they are scattered and fight individually, or in smaller groups. They hide behind bushes, duck down in the high grass, or behind trees and tree stumps. They also lie concealed by roads and fields, which are used by their foes, and when they believe they can strike a target, then they will fire, or shoot their arrows at their enemy. When necessary, they pull back, but if they dare to, they will fall upon the dead and wounded and take scalps, or captives. During a siege, they cut off all approaches to whoever they had surrounded, kill the cattle and closely guard the wells, so as to force a fort to give up, or starve its inhabitants one by one. At night, they hide near the entrance to the gate of a fort, ready to attack the first person who shows himself in the morning. During the day, if there is any kind of cover, such as high grass, a bush, a pile of earth, or a stone hardly as big as a shovel, then they will make use of it, as they crawl on their belly to get within rifle-shot, and whoever appears, will then receive a bullet from their flintlock, whereupon the attacker will disappear in the gun smoke. At other times, they approach the walls of a fort, or the palisades with the greatest bravery with the intention of setting the place on fire, or to smash the gate in. Often, they shoot, or attack at a section of the fort for the purpose of drawing the forces to that point, while they will then, if possible, launch a surprise attack at another point. When they run out of food, which is entirely the responsibility of the individual, their supply is quickly supplemented by a small hunting party. They thereupon rejoin the siege in the hopes of some way obtaining a scalp."

That was the enemy which avenged Kentucky at that time, and with which the early adventurers had to do battle. In battle the Indians were brave; in defeat they were cunning; and in victory they were horrific. Neither sex, age, not even prisoners were taken into consideration and spared by their tomahawks and scalping knives. They saw their eternal enemies take possession of their hunting grounds - the source of their pleasure, their sustenance and their commerce - and they were determined to contest this to the utmost of their abilities.

If they would have had the experience of putting their forces together and then directed their entire united strength against each fort one at a time - of which there were only a few and which were weakly guarded - they then would have easily rid Kentucky of its new settlers, and returned

Kentucky back to the buffalo herds and the Indians. However, fate would have it not.

After they had caused a great deal of grief to the settlers without, however, having been able to conquer even one of their forts, they then withdrew as winter drew near. Before so doing, they had killed many settlers, as well as most of the livestock. However, it must be said of the settlers that they had been hardened by the experience they had endured, and they had acquired a degree of skill in being able to successfully resist the pressure that had been applied to them.

At times, when a fort was in the most dire straits, the Indians would frequently withdraw in order to obtain food, or to take up a position that would be more secure. They usually moved at night, and camped some distance away. This would be at the time when the whites would plow the fields, plant corn, collect the herd scattered in the woods, bring in the harvest, or hunt deer, bear or buffalo, so as to build up a food supply.

"When traveling the settlers avoided the path, and in order to leave, or get back to a fort, they would usually travel at night. Hence, they often had to exchange fire with the Indians, and often when they approached a fort, they found it besieged by Indians. "[6]

In spite of these dangers and difficulties, which the struggle for survival presented them with in the wilderness, and in spite of the Indians lurking around who killed whenever they could, the settlers did not give an inch in terms of giving up their settlements. And when in fall of 1777 Col. Baumann (Bowman) arrived with a hundred men from Virginia for the defense of the settlers, there arose in the heart of the settlers an almost irrepressible hope for a new beginning, a hope that had almost vanished.

In 1778, the courage of the settlers rose even more as a result of the brilliant and successful campaign of Col. George Rogers Clark against the British forts Kaskaskia and Vincennes, and the defeat of the overwhelming forces of Indians and Canadians under Duquesne against Fort Boonesborough.[7] Thereafter, the settlers of Kentucky felt that they were now rightly in possession of the land.

Now the settlers again began to stream into Kentucky. Countless stations were founded in the Blue Grass region, including Lexington, which was established by Col. Robert Patterson and others in April 1779. Patterson was at the time quartered at the station at Harrodsburg, and received the order there to set up a fort north of the Kentucky River. At the head of 25 men, he marched in the direction of the excellent site, where he had been encamped four years earlier with McConnell, Steiner, Hagen, Kenton, and others.

The splendid place with the freshly sparkling spring water was again found. The water sprang forth brightly and clearly and provided the pioneers with such a pleasant drink that Patterson momentarily decided that the fort he had been commissioned to build should be located at this site. In the early morning of 1 April 1779, the axes of this strong party were set in motion, so that the woods resounded with the echo of their blows.

The gigantic trees swiftly fell under the mighty blows of these industrious men, and soon a pleasant square had been cleared, in whose midst a sturdy loghouse surrounded by palisades was constructed. Within its walls the small garrison would be housed for the defense of the area. The first inhabitants of the loghouse were Col. Patterson, John Maxwell, James Masterson, William and Alexander McConnell, Jacob Parberry (Parberg?) and James and Joseph Lindsay.[8] They then planted in the same location a field for the coming winter, which was the same place where the county courthouse now stands.

After Col. John Bowman undertook his unsuccessful expedition against the Shawnee near the Scioto and made the loghouse in Lexington his headquarters, many new settlers arrived, among them several Germans. There were also German participants in the expedition, including: Captain Johann Holder, Major Georg Michael Bedinger, who also functioned as Bowman's Adjutant, Lt. Johannes Hagen of Ruddles Station, Hans Sauter, and Johann Pleakenstalver (Blickenstalwer?)

After the return of the expedition, most of them settled in the Blue Grass region. The immigration especially grew in this year, because in March 1780 the settler's law of Virginia came to an end, which had entitled settlers to 400 acres, and many wanted to secure land, so the number of settlements grew near Boonesborough, Harrodsburg, and other settlements.[9] Some of the bravest settled around a loghouse, which bore the name Lexington, others founded Bryan's Station (1779), which was located about five miles away, under the direction of William Bryan.

This fort lay hardly half a rifle shot away from the rather lonely and poorly constructed road, which led from Harrodsburg to Maysville, and was located on the southern shore of the Elkhorn River. The fort had about forty loghouses, whose inhabitants farmed the surrounding land and hunted in the vicinity of the fort as well. Somewhat distant from the fort, located at the northwestern edge of the forest, there was a clearly sparkling spring, which provided the settlers with fresh water, and by the way, there already was in 1780 a newly constructed and roomy loghouse with its front facing the road, between the spring and the Elkhorn. This was located about a rifle shot north of the fort, or hardly a hundred steps from the northern edge of the fort.

The friendly-looking garden, through which the little stream of the spring flowed to the Elkhorn, was freshly laid out, and announced that the inhabitants of this lonely home placed a higher value on good taste than was usually the case with frontier settlers. This quaint and well organized farm reaching back to the pioneer days of Kentucky was owned by a German, Jacob Böhler, who had settled down here with his youngest son, Johann, and his two beautiful young daughters. He had lost his two other sons in the struggle for freedom from England at the Battle of Brandywine, for which reason he sought a peaceful home in Kentucky far from the fields of the American Revolution.

He had come to Philadelphia as a boy with his parents in 1745 from their homeland in the Rhenish Palatinate.[10] Böhler was about fifty years old, with a strong, imposing and muscular stature. In his face there was an expression of philosophical calm and resignation, which neither pain, nor joy could move out of its equilibrium. In forthrightness, good spirit, and industriousness, he would probably be considered the foremost example of an upright German.

As his parents had been swindled of everything they had in Amsterdam, he had been sold into indentured servitude upon arrival in Philadelphia, and acquired by a well-to-do German farmer, who resided in the Lancaster area.[11] The Moravian missionary Spangenberg took him out of this service as a travel companion on his journey to the Indians in western Pennsylvania.[12] The boy, courageous and of adventurous spirit, gladly followed the Moravian and his comrades. By means of his loyal devotion and willingness to be of service, he fully justified the trust Spangenberg had placed in this open, honest, and modest youth.

Under Spangenberg's direction, he not only learned the teaching of the *New Testament* in accordance with Moravian theology, but other useful subjects as well, including the language of the Shawnee and Delaware

(Indian tribes which at that time lived in western Pennsylvania, but then in the latter third of the 18th century moved into eastern Ohio).[13]

That such a man was a welcome and respected addition to Kentucky at that time, goes without saying. Philipp Niederland and Balthasar Kurz were his closest friends, both of whom lived at Bryan's Station. The history of these Germans, and the attack of the Indians on Bryan's Station under the direction of the infamous Simon Girty was described in a novel by Samuel Maclea, who edited the *Didaskia* in Baltimore in 1848.[14]

The descendants of Böhler, Kurz, and Niederwald still live in the Blue Grass region, although their names have been Anglicized as: Baylor, Short, and Netherland.[15] A W. Baylor was named by Governor Garrard as one of the commissioners with Johann A. Seitz to copy the partially destroyed books at the courthouse. Georg W. Baylor was a state representative in 1817-18, as was E. Baylor in 1819, both of whom were from Bourbon County.[16]

Notes

1. Flint, *Life of Boone*, p. 85; Collins, 2nd Edition, Vol. II, p. 526; Butler, p. 32. HAR.

2. Hinkston's Station, in present day Harrison County, Kentucky, was founded in 1775 by Johannes Hinkston, Johannes Hagen, Johann Martin, and 13 others, and took its name from the leader of this party. Some times it was called Martin's Station. Several days after the arrival of the so-called Hinkston party a second group came down the Ohio River in canoes, the so-called Miller party, which then united with the former at the lower Blue Lick. To this group belonged the brothers Wilhelm and Hans Müller and Johannes Schier (Shear). Both parties came from Pennsylvania. In the following year (1776), the following Pennsylvania Germans arrived: Johann Hagen, Wilhelm Müller, Hans Müller, Wilhelm Bays, Wilhelm Markland, and others. And in the next year, they were joined by: the brothers Isaac and Jacob Ruddel, Nicolaus Hart, Samuel Vanhook and Johann Burger. The fort which they built on the northern shore of the South Licking River, was now known as Ruddel's Station, as the one built by the Hinkston groups had been destroyed by the Indians. Collins, Vol. II, pp. 21, 324-28. HAR.

3. Collins, 2nd Edition, Vol. I, p. 19. HAR.

4. H. A. Rattermann, *Geschichte des Grossen Nordamerikanischen Westens*, Vol. I, p. 53. HAR.

5. According to a letter of Col. Floyd; Butler, *History of Kentucky*, p. 31. HAR

6. Butler, pp. 33-35. HAR.

7. Major Clark, with 153 men in four companies divided unter the command of Captains Baumann (Bowman), Leonard Helm, Wilhelm Harrod and Joseph Montgomery, among which were the well-known backwoodsmen Simon Kenton and Johannes Hagen (Haggin), left the camp located at the Falls of the Ohio toward mid-June 1778, traveled with keelboats up the Ohio River until they were a small stretch above the location where Fort Massac was located later, and from here on land to

Kaskaskia. They surprised this fort the night of 4 July without firing a rifle shot. Raynold, *The Pioneer History of Illinois*, pp. 70-75; Rattermann, *Geschichte des Grossen Westens*, Vol. I, pp. 57-61. HAR.

8. Ranck, pp. 23-24; Collins, Vol. II, p. 180. HAR.

9. Filson, *Discovery, Settlement and Present State of Kentucky*, p. 32. HAR.

10. Regarding the immigration of the Palatines in the 18th century, see Don Heinrich Tolzmann, ed., *German Immigration to America: The First Wave*. (Bowie, MD: Heritage Books, Inc., 1993). DHT.

11. For further information on indentured servitude and the German immigration, see Don Heinrich Tolzmann, ed., *The Pennsylvania Germans: Jesse Leonard Rosenberger's Sketch of Their History and Life*. (Bowie, MD: Heritage Books, Inc., 1998). DHT.

12. Spangenberg was the leader of the Moravian Church in America. See Lucy F. Bittinger, *The Germans in Colonial Times*. (Philadelphia: J.B. Lippincott, 1901). DHT.

13. For a report on the Ohio territory by a German Moravian missionary, see Don Heinrich Tolzmann, ed., *The First Description of Cincinnati and other Ohio Settlements: The Travel Report of Johann Heckewelder, 1792*. (Lanham, MD: University Press of America, 1988). DHT.

14. Maclea's publication itself would be worthy of further examination.

15. German names were commonly Anglicized, or misspelled in the colonial period. Common examples with their Anglicized variants are: Baumann/Bowman; Baehr/Bear; and Schmidt/Smith. See George Fenwick Jones, *German-American Names*. 2nd Edition. (Baltimore: Genealogical Publishing Co., 1995). DHT.

16. Collins, Vol. II, pp. 173, 772. HAR.

3. In and Around Lexington

After the construction of the loghouse in Lexington, the permanent settlement of the place began. The pioneers came from all side, and soon began work of clearing the forest. Loghouses arose here and there in the midst of the forest, and soon corn and potato fields were planted throughout the scattered clearings. Civilization made its entrance.

Life in the backwoods was certainly more picturesque than comfortable and pleasant. Men had to take turns standing on guard, as the Indians continually harassed the settlers while they worked. Those who traversed the forest in hunting parties were in constant danger of being shot and scalped. However, those who didn't stand guard, but rather were engaged in duties at home, or cleared the forest, plowed, planted, harvested, etc., were also in danger. Lurking behind a tree there could be an Indian lying in wait to take a scalp. Even the women were not free of danger for their lives. They also were killed and scalped by the Indians while milking cows, while harvesting corn or grain, just like their male counterparts.

The only reason why the settlers had left the parts of the country already settled earlier and come over the mountains, was the search for cheap land, and this was, as the saying goes, there for the taking. It was, however, understood, that it was necessary to build a loghouse, and to bring in a harvest of crops, so that one could then obtain title to 400 acres of land.

Also, one could obtain the right to purchase an additional 1,000 acres of land in the area. This could be obtained by means of a land warrant. This was in accordance with the laws of Virginia, and as noted earlier, this law came to an end in 1780. However, settlers continued with the practice in spite of the fact that the law had been discontinued, which led to frequent confrontations, in which settlers came into armed conflict with those who had purchased land.

One way in which settlers took possession of land was known as "Tomahawk Rights" This occurred as several trees near a spring were killed by "girdling" them, and then the initials of the settler were carved into the bark. Such land titles were valid until a new law was passed in 1781, which overturned such land claims. Nonetheless, attempts were still made with such land claims. Therefore, the so-called "strait-jacket" practice took effect to deal with such claims, whereby such claimants donned a jacket and took a whipping with a freshly cut hickory stick, whereupon such Tomahawk-claimants became ever more rare.

Most settlers considered the land as only of slight value, because they thought it would lose its fruitfulness in a few years. Here they made a major mistake and the Germans among them soon cleared up such foolishness. Several settlers came west in the spring - leaving their families in the east - and planted, first of all, a small cornfield, prepared to build a loghouse, so as to then bring their families in the fall. Others, whose families were not very large, brought them along already in the spring. It then frequently happened that their supply of flour, which was mainly Indian corn meal, often ran out, which meant that the family was out of bread and cornmeal.

To replace this, dry deer meat and turkey breast was used as bread, and only bear meat was called meat. Such alternatives meant, however, little to the human system, and one's stomach felt empty regardless of what you called it. As a result, a number of illnesses frequently occurred. Children, who lacked the necessary basic foods, shriveled up and appeared pale and sickly. No wonder that they longed for the harvest of the potatoes, pumpkins, and squash. How delicious the first potatoes tasted, and what joy reigned when the first ear of corn was harvested.

And even if this corn was hard to grind on a grinding iron, then how good the baked Johnny cakes tasted. This was a real festive occasion for the children, and they again thrived and became healthy and strong, their cheeks became rosy again and a sublime satisfaction reigned in the homes of the pioneers, regardless of how poor their homes appeared.

The home utensils of the first settlers were neither countless, nor expensive. Tables and beds were the essentials, and the tableware consisted of a few tin plates and spoons, but not always! At times, there were wooden bowls, plates and vessels. Aside from wooden dishware, there was also some made out of hollowed out pumpkin or squash gourds. Iron pots, knives, and forks were rare and usually had to be brought by packhorse over the mountain. Instead of chairs one used a block of wood, and only rarely did one find well made benches, or actual chairs.

This housing material harmonized perfectly with the food. Corn porridge and bacon were the usual daily meal. Johnny cakes in the beginning were the only real kind of bread available. Johnny cakes and bacon, or when this was not available, bear and deer meat would be for breakfast; lunch consisted of beans, potatoes, and other vegetables, and in summer roast corn as well; and for the evening meal there also was corn and milk. If a log rolling or house raising took place, than there was a festive meal of pot pie. The pioneers had as little coffee or tea, as they did silver and porcelain.

As simple as they were with regard to food, so too were they simple in dress. Only self-woven materials were used. They were either linen or half wool. With men, who frequently were hunting, the clothing was half Indian. A hunting shirt was worn everywhere. It was a kind of loose jacket that hung halfway down to the hips, with the chest open so wide that a pair of hands would fit in place when the belt was tied.

The sleeves were wide and open on the ends. The collar was wide and made out of some homemade sewn material and of a different color than the shirt. The opening at the chest served as a kind of garment sack where one could store some bread or cakes, or carry a cloth for the cleaning of a rifle, or some other object or item. The belt served to hold the clothing together, as well as for other purposes. In front, one carried a bullet pouch and one's gloves, on the right side a tomahawk and on the left a scalping knife in a leather sheath. The hunting shirt was mostly of half woolen material, more rare was that made of linen, and also of deer skin.

A pair of pantaloons served to cover the hips and legs, and instead of shoes or boots one wore moccasins. These served the feet better than modern shoes. They were made of tanned dear skin, and were of one piece, and seamed in front and at the heel, and reached on one's legs halfway up the calf. They were tied tight with leather straps. The moccasins for everyday use could be made in a few hours.

The only tools available for making tableware were a knife and an awl, which was usually made out of a folding knife. Such an awl usually had a deerhorn handle and a roll of deer skin for the repair of moccasins, both of which hung together in a thronged sack. The making of moccasins was usually an evening-time task. In the cold winter, moccasins with deer fur or dry foliage kept your feet warm. With wet weather it was said that wearing moccasins was a nice way to go barefoot. This was true, as the porous deer skin is not water repellant. This poor kind of footwear contributed to the fact that many a hunter and frontiersman later suffered from rheumatism. They became well aware of this and at night would try to hold their feet in the direction of the fireplace, which helped soothe the pain somewhat.

As a result of Indian warfare, young men came to wear Indian-style clothing. The pants were set aside and the Indian shirts made longer so that they reached down past the hips. An Indian garment was adopted (a piece of half wool cloth and about a yard long and 8-9 inches wide), which was worn in front and back and pulled through one's belt. The same belt, which held the cloth in place, also bore the long leggings, which were bound together by means of strings. When the belt was in place around the hunting shirt, as it often happened, there remained a section of the thigh or hip that was uncovered. The young hunters, however, instead of being ashamed of this, were proud of their Indian attire, and even attended church in this fashion. If their appearance increased the piety of the young women is another question.

Half woolen undergarments and the so-called bed-gown, which was then the customary clothing of women, would be looked at as something unusual today. A small self-woven neck scarf - all women spun and wove at that time - would most likely not replace the elegantly made ones which adorn the necks of ladies today. At that time, pioneer women went barefoot during warm weather; in the winter, they wore moccasins, or some coarsely made shoes, which in comparison to the elegant slippers our wives and daughters wear today would be ridiculous. The clothes of women as well as men were hung on wooden hooks on the walls of the loghouses, and as such took the place of hung tapestries, but also immediately showed visitors the wealth of the home's inhabitants, at least in terms of their clothing.

The dressing-table of our ladies replaces the pioneers' spinning wheel, weaver's loom, sickle, and hoe! However, they were always happy and of good spirit, and satisfied when they had received half woolen dresses and could cover their heads with a sunbonnet of coarse linen.

The spring of 1780 could be viewed as a period of testing for the pioneers of the Blue Grass region, and one of heroic endurance. Already in the early days of spring, the Indians began to attack the area where the settlers were located. And as summer approached, the attacks continued, and hunting parties had to flee to the fort. One of the settlers by the name of Weimer, who dared out on his own, was killed by the Indians and scalped, and a young man, who went out to gather the cattle from the woods, was mortally wounded, and chased to the gate of the fort. His bride, a courageous young women, opened the gate and dragged her wounded husband into the fort in spite of the fact that the Indians were only a few steps from her. The young man died a few minutes later in the arms of his courageous wife.[1]

In May, the Indians attacked Strode's Station, located in the vicinity of present day Winchester, and in June they appeared in great number before the fort at Lexington. However, they did not attack, but rather were content in taking all the horses and cattle of the settlers from the nearby woods, and in setting fire to the cornfields, after which they disappeared. The fort was astonished at the inexplicable sudden disappearance of the Indians, as they thought the Indians were giving up, and their astonishment was heightened when they heard cannon shots in the distance, the first that had ever been heard in the forests of "dark and bloody" Kentucky.

Full of worry, the resolute group stood on guard at the fort, with loaded rifles at hand anxiously waiting to learn what the unexpected canon fire might mean. Then one day, Captain Hinkston, who had fled from the Indians, appeared and notified the fort of the news of the fall of Ruddell's and Martin's Stations, which had been taken by the British Col. Byrd with a force of English troops and Indians. The atrocities of the Indians on this occasion held Byrd off from proceeding against Lexington and Bryant's Station. He then returned to Detroit and with him withdrew the Indians for this year.

As it had by now been decided to establish a city around the loghouse, it was viewed as advisable to establish a greater degree of defense than was provided by the loghouse fort. Three other loghouses were built and connected together by means of palisades. On the long sides of this rectangular fort more loghouses were built for supplies etc., and in the middle a row of homes was constructed. The fort embraced the spring mentioned earlier, so that this would be protected in the case of an attack by an invading force.

In the meantime, the population increased substantially, and in the fall of 1781 the following trustees were named to lay out the city: H. McIlvain, Robert Patterson, James Hughes, Alexander Parker, Johannes A. Seitz, Georg Tegersen, Thomas January, and James Morrison. On 26 December of the year, they reported on the plan for the city, which was laid out in regular squares.

On the same day, 62 building lots were sold to the following Germans: Nikolaus Brobsten, Wilhelm Martinsen., and his three sons, Johannes, H. and Samuel, Johannes and Wilhelm Niblich, Karl Seemann, Joseph Weller, and Johannes Weimar. In the years 1782-83, the following Germans settled in Lexington: Christopher Kistner and his mother Georg Schäfer, Bernard Niederland and his brothers, Adam, Jacob, and Christopher Zumwald.

Major Bernard Niederland, mentioned the foregoing list of first property owners in Lexington, was born of German parents in Powhaton, County, Virginia on 27 February 1755. During the American Revolution, he had served under General Lincoln in the southern army, and was captured during the siege of Savannah, as he served under the Swiss Lt. Fleland as an attempt was made to storm the walls. He was held prisoner for ten months. He then managed somehow to escape, but was later captured and sent to San Augustin, Florida, where the British had stations for their navy.

He escaped again and made his way to Beaufort in South Carolina, where he again joined the American forces. In fall 1781, he came to Kentucky, and settled down in Lexington Station and became one of the most prominent men in the frontier wars of the time. Later, he moved to Jessamine County, where he died in October 1838, and was provided with a military burial.[2] His oldest brother, Philipp Niederland, also came with him to Kentucky, and later settled in Bourbon County.

In Bourbon County Captain Johannes Waller settled down in ca. 1784. He had been a member of a group which Simon Kenton had also belonged to, which in 1775 had built the first loghouse at Lawrence Creek in the vicinity of Maysville. Of this party only the names of Hans Waller and Simon Kenton have been preserved. The place where the loghouse was built was at that time named Drennon's Spring.[3]

As there were so many Indians in the area, the place was then abandoned. Waller, however, returned in December 1784 and brought his father, Eduard Waller, who was known as "Old Ned." The elder Waller was one of the early settlers of Germanna, in Spotsylvania County, Virginia. This almost exclusively German settlement had been established by Governor Spotswood, and consisted mainly of Lutherans from northern Germany.

Due to the favorable conditions they held to the Anglican Church, although their German ministers were all of the Lutheran Confession. After a number of Anabaptists settled in Germanna in 1768, the local clergy began to harass them, with the support of Waller. He was then arrested on 4 June 1768 by a number of persons, and led to a court consisting of three justices of the peace, found guilt of breaking the peace, and sentenced to jail.[4] Later, the Wallers, father and son, again came into conflict with the authorities, as a result of which they left the Shenandoah Valley.

They settled down at the upper waters of the Opequon, where many Germans and Irish had settled. Here the young Waller met Simon Kenton, and came with him to Kentucky. Both of the Wallers and Georg Lewis are the real founders of Maysville, which was known as Limestone Point until 1800. In 1784, Hans Waller and Johannes Müller moved to the Middle Fork of the Licking River, in the vicinity of the upper Blue Lick. They settled down about 13 miles south of Blue Lick Springs, and built here the well-known settlement known as Miller's Station. Here there arose the settlement of Millersburg at Hinkston Creek.[5]

Notes

1.Ranck, pp. 34-35. HAR.

2.Ranck, pp. 100-101. HAR. Regarding German-Americans in the Revolutionary War, see Don Heinrich Tolzmann, ed, *The German-American Soldier in the Wars of the U.S.: J.G. Rosengarten's History*. (Bowie, MD: Heritage Books, Inc., 1996). DHT.

3. McDonald, *The Life of Simon Kenton*, p . 250; "Depositions of John Waller," in: *Mason County Court Records*. (15 July 1797; 30 Nov. 1804).

4. Kercheval, *History of the Valley of Virginia*, p. 55. HAR. For further information on the German settlement at Germanna, Virginia, see Tolzmann, ed., *The German Element in Virginia*, Vol. I, pp. 60ff. DHT.

5. Collins writes (Vol. II, p. 66) that Millersburg was established in 1817, which is, however, an error, as F. Cummings writes as follows of Millersburg in 1807: "We breakfasted at Capt. Waller's tavern at Millersburgh. Our host was an obliging and sensible man, and possesses of general information relative to this Country: he was not destitute of some particulars also. We collected from him, that when he first arrived in (Millersburgh) Kentucky about twenty-three years ago, there was not a house between Limestone and Lexington, and at the latter place were only a few log-cabins under the protection of a staccato fort." See Cumming, *Sketches of a Tour to the Western Country*. (Pittsburgh, 1810), p. 156. HAR.

4. The Battle at Blue Lick

In the vicinity of Millersburg, one of bloodiest battles in the history of Kentucky took place. In August 1782, a group of Shawnees led by Simon Girty arrived with the goal of driving the "long knives" out of Kentucky. In the following account, the author draws on his history of the American West, *Geschichte des Nordamerikanischen Westens*, where he described the battle in detail.

On 14 August 1782, about 600 Indians arrived near Bryan's Station at the Elkhorn River, which was being defended by 50 men. There were also some settlers there, as the frontier had become unsafe, and there were about 40 loghouses within the fort where they could stay. The fort itself was strongly built with a mighty palisade fence around it. This was surrounded by a pit about 4-5 feet deep. At each of the four corners there was a substantial loghouse, which served to stave off any advance of the Indians and any attempt they would make to start a fire. Therefore, the fort was quite secure against any attempt to scale its walls, as well as any attack in general, with the exception, of course, of cannon fire.

A serious mistake, however had been made in its construction in that it had not been built around a nearby spring, which was located outside the walls of the fort. If the Indians had been more careful, they would have succeeded in capturing the fort. On the morning of 15 August, when several people wanted to get water, they were fired upon, and it was thereby discovered that there was a sizable party of Indians hiding in the woods. The news was quickly sent to Lexington with the request for help, and the messenger made it through the Indians without getting discovered, or captured. However, now the settlers lacked water.

The Indians, about 500 strong, had hidden themselves in the woods by the spring, and in the meantime sent a group of 100 warriors to attack the southeast corner of the fort as a feint attack. The Commandant of the fort recognized the situation, and called the women of the fort together, and explained the need for water, especially if the attack would soon begin, as thereafter there would be no chance of getting any. He then requested that they all go to the spring and fill their pales with water. He did not conceal the fact that he felt that there were Indians laying in wait in the woods nearby. Several women protested then that they were being asked to get water at such a dangerous time, and that it would be better if men went out for the water, and that the Indians would not care if they killed and scalped men or women.

They were then told that it was the women who usually got the water, and if they would go to get it as usual, then the Indians would think they had not been discovered, and would not disturb them. However, if men came out, then that would be a sign that their presence had been discovered, and they would have to give up their plan of attacking the fort, and would shoot the men down and try to storm the gates of the fort. This decided the question.

Several of the most courageous women now declared that they would go to the spring without fear, and some of the younger and less brave ones then joined in also. They all then headed towards the spring, or right into the sight of the rifles of 500 Indian warriors. some of the young women could hardly overcome their fear, but the older women went forth with such firmness and a sense of calm that the Indians were completely fooled. Not a shot was fired. They filled their pales with water, and even if they began to walk a bit faster on the return trip, and even almost finally got into a unmilitary kind of gallop, which developed into a throng at the gate, still they had hardly spilled a drop of water.

Now the Indian attack on the fort began. Twice they tried to storm the fort, but were met with a determined storm of bullets, which promptly met them and sent them back into the woods with many losses. on the next day, they fort received reinforcements from Lexington, which made it into the fort with few losses. In the evening, Girty tried to move the fort to capitulate, and threatened that cannons were on the way, but the courageous fort refused to fall for this.

Night passed as an uninterrupted interlude, and at daybreak, they discovered that the Indians had left their camp, The campfires were still burning and several pieces of meat were still roasting in the fire, which led one to conclude that they had left shortly before dawn.

Early in the morning the reinforcements began to arrive and by midday, 167 men were there, including Col. Boone, Todd, Triggs, and many others. A war council was held, and it was decided to follow the Indians, although their number was about one-fourth the size of the Indian force. On the following day, they succeeded in locating the Indians. Col. Boone advised that they should wait until Col. Logan and his forces arrived, but Major McGary, who not known for being able to tame his daringness, called out in a manner mimicking the Indian battle-cry: "He who is not a coward, follow me!"

This had a magic effect, and without plan or order they all stormed into the attack on the Indians, who were hidden in the woods. They were met with a murderous firestorm from their rifles and in a matter of a few minutes, the troops had been almost entirely cut down. The Indians then sprung from their hiding places and fell on the troops with their scalping knives and a horrible slaughter then followed. Col. Boone and a few of his best friends barely were able to escape, but as they knew the land well, and because they made it through one of the ravines where the Indians had hidden before the attack.

The sad news of the Battle of Blue Lick spread throughout the colony and the entire country grieved at the losses, as it was the greatest defeat Kentucky had ever suffered. 60 men had been killed and scalped and a great number had been captured. The loss of the Indians at the battle was significant, but not in relation to those of the settlers.

In the evening of the last, Col. Logan arrived in Bryan's Station with 450 men. As he sensed a problem, he swiftly marched ahead and met the advance party of those fleeing the battle. After receiving the sad news, he continued his pursuit in haste and arrived on the next day at the battle site. The enemy was gone, but what a horrible sight they found. On he battle field he found the corpses of the Kentuckians where they had fallen.

Many circles of buzzards flew overhead and in the river the bodies of dead men and horses were found caught up in the bushes and trees . The corpses had swollen up greatly and due to the warm sunlight had already begun to decay, so that the fish were already nibbling on them. The corpses were carefully collected and buried, whereupon the troops returned to Lexington, as the Indians had escaped.

Regarding the bravery of Bernard Niederland at this battle McClung wrote as follows: "A man by the name of Niederland, who had earlier been suspected of cowardice, demonstrated a coolness and thoughtfulness that was equally noble as unexpected. He was an excellent horseman, and had ridden ahead to the fleeing troops. About 20 other riders followed him across the river, and as the river was between them and the enemy, they aimed to go ahead without any concern as to the security of their friends in those crossing the river who were not on horse.

Niederland stopped his horse and called out for all to halt, and to save those in the river. The group obeyed, stopped, and fired a salvo in the rear guard of the enemy, which thereupon retreated from the place. This then provided the necessary time to rescue those in need to the other side of the river."[1] Aside from Niederland the names of those in the battle were: Jesse Yocum (Joachim), Ludwig Rose, Major Georg Michael Bedinger, Peter Harget, and 29 others.

Major Bedinger was born in 1755 of German parents in Schaefersdorf, Virginia. When he was 24, he came to Boonesborough. He was a member of a party of 10, including: Johann Holder, Thomas Schwearingen and Joseph Doniphan, who settled at Muddy Creek in Mason County, Kentucky, in order to clear some land there. In May 1779, he served under Col. Johann Baumann as adjutant during the unsuccessful campaign to old Chillicothe. At the Battle of Blue Lick, 19 August 1782, he served as a major. In 1792, he was elected to the state legislature from Bourbon County, and from 1803-07, he was a member of Congress. He died on 7 December 1843 at his home at the lower Blue Lick in present day Nicholas County, Kentucky.[2]

Notes

1. See Rattermann, *Geschichte* Vol. I, p. 85. HAR.

2. According the *Dictionary of American Biography*, Bedinger was a "Revolutionary soldier, early Kentucky settler, and opponent of slavery. DHT.

5. Lexington's First Germans

In January 1783, Kentucky was raised to the status of an independent court district by the legislature of Virginia. The judges appointed for this district met in Harrodsburg on 3 March 1783, and decided to move the court to Danville. The seat of government remained in this somewhat out-of-the-way county of the Old Dominion until 1792, when Kentucky was admitted to the Union.[1] The first judges of this court were: John Floyd, Samuel McDowell, and Georg Muter.

The latter, son of a German father and Scottish mother, was born in Madison County, Virginia, and played an important role in the organizational history of Kentucky. He was a member of the Kentucky convention aimed at the establishment of a state in May 1785, August 1785, 1787, and 1788. He also served as an elector from Woodford County in 1792, and was elected 28 June 1792 judge of the state supreme court (Court of Oyer and Terminer). Later, he was censured by the legislature for his decision in the land claim of McConnell vs. Simon Kenton, as he decided against the tenuous land grants of Virginia, and in favor of the strict enforcement of land laws.

As most of the land titles in Kentucky were rendered illegal by means of this decision, many were quite displeased with this decision. The legislature attempted to depose Judges Muter and Sebastian, which, however, failed. After they modified their decision in a later judgement, Muter retired from office in 1795. In 1806, the legislature granted him a pension for services rendered to Kentucky, which, however, was revoked in 1809. This negative act on the part of the state legislature related completely to party politics. So as to make this clear, one of the most important events in the history of the state has to be described in greater detail.

The inhabitants of young Kentucky, cut off from the eastern states through rugged and immovable mountain regions, without any other trade routes than over the primitive paths hewn through the woods, naturally sought to sell the produce of the land, not only for the acquisition of the necessary tools, but for the other items they desired. The Mississippi was the only viable trade route, in their view. However, the lower part of the river was in the hands of the Spaniards, which closed off commerce on the river.

The Kentuckians demanded that the federal government establish a trade agreement, which would open the river up to free commerce. Congress, however, had nothing but deaf ears for the western settlers, as the Easterners wanted to exploit the West for their own purposes, as is still the case today. And so the attempt to open up the Mississippi to trade was a failure, and this especially due to Ambassador Jay.

Even the administration of Washington had considered it advisable to keep the river trade closed, so as to keep the westerners bound to the eastern states. To replace the option of a trade route on the Mississippi, Washington suggested a connection between the Ohio River with the James River and the Potomac by means of a canal system. That this could only raise the dissatisfaction of the westerners, became immediately apparent.

The colonists in the West were in need of swift and speedy assistance, and did not want to get involved in a gigantic project, which would be completed by the time their grandchildren had arrived. However, as noted earlier, the eastern politicians were completely blind and deaf to the interests of the westerners.[2]

The Ambassador of France, Richard Genee, tried to exploit this in the interests of French policy. In November 1793, his agents, Lachaise, Delpeau, Mathurin, and Gignoux, appeared in Kentucky complete with commissions to set up a military movement against the Spanish holdings on the lower Mississippi, as well as to establish an independent republic in the West. Many of those who had been repelled by the federal government's lack of interest, became interested in this prospect, and joined in the plan.

Even the patriotic general George Rogers Clark was motivated to accept a patent as General Major of the Armies of France and Supreme Commander of the Revolutionary Legions of the Mississippi. The Kentuckians demanded above all else, the rights of free commerce on the Mississippi, either through the federal government, or through the establishment of a separate government in the West. That they thereby were engaging in treason, did not readily occur to them, as at that time (1791) Vermont was not even part of the Union.

Democratic clubs, like the French Jacobin clubs, were being founded everywhere. In the summer 1793, three such clubs were formed in Kentucky, in: Lexington, Georgetown, and Paris. Their spirit was decidedly anti-federalist. Free commerce on the Mississippi, the Accise law, the Indian wars, the timidity of Congress in relation to England, and the denigration of the former ally, France, in the desperate hour of its struggle against all the despots of Europe, formed the basis of the most hotly contested debates in these organizations, as well as of the population at large in general.

No wonder that Washington's requests to the Governor of Kentucky, Shelby, that these clubs be declared treasonous, were only met with scorn. Meetings were called and resolutions passed, in which the greatest bitterness against the federal government were expressed.[3] Other demonstrations took place, in which they wildest passions were unleashed.

So the effigy of John Jay, who had just been appointed by Washington as Ambassador to England, was burned in Lexington on 31 May 1794 during one such meeting. The stuffed effigy had an iron switch in one hand and in the other a scroll with the inscription : "Nemo repente fuit turpissimus." *Juven. Sat.*. V. 33 (No one else rises immediately to such vice); and on the other side: "Non deficit alter," *Virg. Aen.* (Another of this kind is not desired). Around its head there hung on a noose a copy of John Adams, *Defense of the American Constitution*. On its cover was written: "Scribere jussit aurum," *Ovid. Ep.* (Gold made me write it). After the figure had been shown hanging out of the window of a German barber, Martin Kassel, it was taken by the large mob, decapitated, and burned. As it contained a packet of gunpowder, it then exploded the great delight of the public.

The whole history of French intrigue gradually dissolved in the sand later Ambassador Genet was recalled in 1795, and was only completely settled when Louisiana was purchased by France and was then ceded to the U.S.

Even if he tried to exert a peaceful influence, it was noticed by Kentuckians that Muter had in 1809 joined the Federalist party. After the Republicans were victorious and the votes of Kentucky for President Madison were presented, Muter was then deprived of his pension. So it can only be surmised that this revocation in that year had something to do with the politics of the time. Muter was generally well-loved, and the historian Butler writes of him that there never was a milder, more worthy, and respected man.

A characteristic of Muter, which strikes us, is his active involvement in community affairs in Lexington. He was a member of the German and Lutheran Reformed Church of Lexington, and also member of first president of the Caledonian Society, in which he proudly proclaimed his ethnic heritage. Otherwise, Muter was an exceptional jurist and a learned man. In 1789, he was one of the main founders of the Society for the Dissemination of Useful Knowledge. He died in Lexington in 1811.[4]

Lexington in the 18th century was already not only a commercial center of the West of the day, but also the seat of cultural and intellectual life. The first school dates to 1780. One of the first schoolmasters in Lexington was the Frenchman Jean Filson, who was involved in the founding of Cincinnati. Filson was the author of the life history of Daniel Boone, as well as the first history of Kentucky, which was published in French, as well as English.[5]

The first institution of higher education in the West was founded in Lexington in 1790 as Transylvania Seminary. And among its founders was Judge Muter. David Lietsch also one of the founders. The Seminary became a College in 1798 when it merged with the Kentucky Academy, and was elevated to the status of a university, the first in the West, as Transylvania University. Among the faculty members in this University, which enjoyed a great reputation at that time, we find several respected German scholars, such as Dr. Daniel Mayer, the well-known ethnologist Dr. C. S. Rafinesque, Prof. Johann Lutz, Dr. J.M. Busch, Dr. Johann Eberle, Prof. Benj. Gratz and others.

An Immigration Society was founded in Lexington in 1797, and its first president was Thomas Hart. The society did all to make Lexington a thriving city in the West. It issued circulars and distributed them in the East. They praised the advantages of the Blue Grass region of Kentucky. In one of these circulars, the fertility of the soil was described as follows: The average results of a harvest per acre are: 25 bushels for wheat (on land previously planted with corn), or 35 on new land; corn,60; rye, 25; barley, 40; oats, 40; potatoes, 250; hemp, 8 Centner; tobacco, 1 ton; hay, 3 tons. And the Lexington market price is as follows: for wheat per bushel, $1; corn, 20 Cents; rye, 66 Cents; oats, 17 Cents; barley, 50 Cents; potatoes, 10 Cents; hemp, per ton, $86.66; tobacco, per Centner, $4; hay, per ton, $6.

In another circular, the population of Lexington is indicated as numbering 1,600 in 1797. The number of houses was about 200, and some of them were brick, others wooden, but most of them were still loghouses. A building lot in the city cost $30, and an acre of farmland in the area was $5. These circulars were also translated into German in Philadelphia and

Baltimore and distributed to recently arrived German immigrants. It was, therefore, not surprising that there were many German settlers in and around Lexington before 1800.[6]

The first land register of the region were destroyed in a fire at the courthouse in Lexington, and the oldest book dates to 1796. Among the landholders, who sold land in that year, we find the following German names: Jakob Reybolt, Karl Wilking Jakob Keyser, Adam Hartmann, Johannes Rochus, Peter Kruse, Achilles Helm, Wilhelm Schinn and Thomas Lischmann. Among the buyers of property in and around Lexington we find the following German names: Martin Franks, Edmund Gulion, Simon Lützel, Georg Jung, Franz Kühn, Bernard Lingenfetter, Johannes Gärtner, Georg Poyzer, Daniel Weibel.

Poyzer was an owner of the first dry-goods store in Lexington. He was in partnership with William Macbean, the well-known merchant of Philadelphia, who lent him the necessary capital ($7,099.20 from Macbean and $310.35 from Poyzer). A third partner, who did not contribute any funds was John Anderson, but had the job of selling goods in Kentucky and Tennessee, while Poyzer ran the business in Lexington.

Their contract, on page 122 of the land register A, contains the following stipulations, which shed light on the social conditions of the time: "No partner shall draw more than $300 annually for personal use; none of the partners shall game more than $50; no one should be on bail, nor sign for bail, other than in relation to the business."

It appears that already in the new settlement that the rage for gaming was the desire to gamble was on the upswing. That Germans were among the most passionate players can easily be imagined as their tendency to gaming is one of their characteristics, which was even referred to by Tacitus in his work on the customs and traditions of the early Germans.[7]

Related to this it is noteworthy that the first legally permitted lottery in Kentucky was organized by Germans, and was for the welfare of the founding of a German church in Lexington. On 15 December 1792, the authorities granted the following trustees of the "Dutch Presbyterian Society:" Johannes Schmidt (Smith), Benedict Schwab (Swope), Kaspar Kerstner (Casper Carsner), Martin Kassel (Castle), and Jakob Keyser (Kiser) the permission to sponsor a lottery. The purpose of the lottery was to raise $500 to enable the society to acquire land at Hill Street, between

Mill and Upper Streets.. The funds would also enable them to build a church and school.

In 1795, the first church services were held, but before it even opened it was acquired by the united German Lutheran and Reformed congregation, whose first minster was Rev. Tischmann and a Mr. Löhri served as schoolmaster. The congregation, according to Rank, consisted of Germans, among them the following: Heinrich Lemkert, Jakob Springel, Johannes Keyser, Adam Weber, Georg Adams, Hagert, Eduard Howe, M. Meyer and Mr. Böshardt.[8]

This church was destroyed by fire in 1815 and as a result of a lack of new immigrants and due to the death of the pastor, who was replaced by an English-speaking one, there occurred a schism in the church, and the church was not rebuilt. The lot was later sold to the Methodists, who still maintain a church at that site.

Notes

1. "Old Dominion" is a popular name for the state of Virginia. It probably arose in the following way: In Captain John Smith's history of Virginia (1629) there was a map which referred to all of the British colonies as Virginia. However, to identify what today is Virginia, it is referred to as "auld Virginia" and New England as "new Virginia." As at that time all colonies were officially known as part of the "royal dominion," there, therefore, arose the name "Old Dominion" for the older colony, which was also referred to as "Old Virginia." HAR.

2. Marshall, *History of Kentucky*. 2nd Edition, Vol. I, p. 294; Butler, p. 169. HAR.

3. We would like to include the resolutions passed at a demonstration meeting in Lexington, which was held 24 May 1794 under the direction of Judge Muter, especially because they are found in no other history of Kentucky, but can be found in: *The Centennial of the Northwestern Territory*. (14 June 1794). We have excluded the introduction and resolutions 8 and 9, which were not essential to the conveying the position of the meeting:

"1. Be it resolved that the inhabitants of the land west of the Appalachian Mountains are entitled by nature and stipulations to a free and undisturbed free maritime trade on the Mississippi.

2. That from the year 1783 to the present time this right has been deprived of them by the Spaniards.

3. That the federal government, whose duty it was, to procure this right for us, either intentionally, or by means of an erroneous policy, has taken no effective steps in that direction.

4. That the measures it made use of, were concealed from us.

5. That it is a misuse of the freedom of the citizenry if it is tolerated that the servants of the people may say to their masters that the messages which they consider important are withheld from them.

6. That we have a privilege and right to expect and demand that Spain be forced to recognize our rights immediately, and that all other related discussions in this matter be terminated.

7. That the mishandled affairs and insults, which Britain has accorded America, cry loudly for action, and that we will support the federal government with all our means and strengths in the attempt to attain the rights it deserves.

10. That the inhabitants of the West have a basic right to demand that its borders be protected by the federal government, and the total lack of said protection at the present time is a grievance of the highest importance.

11. That the attainment and security of these rights is in the common interest of the population of the West, and that we are ready to make such of such measures as necessary to further these rights.

12. It is our view that at the moment steps are being taken to obtain the opinions of the people of this state, so that there is no doubt as to their wishes and positions in these important matters, and that we are able as a state to act in concert with other western territories.

13. Therefore, be it resolved that it is recommended to each county in the state to appoint committees, in order to give and receive communications on these matters; to call meetings in their districts; and when it is considered advisable, to ask the people to elect fitting persons, who shall represent them in a meeting of elected representatives, which shall advise on such appropriate steps as should be made to attain and secure unser rights." HAR.

4. Muter appears to have been an early example of what came to be referred to in the 19th century as "the ethnic politician." He appears to have been active in community affairs, and made his of his ethnicity for political purposes. This, of course, was later perfected by Schurz. See Hans L. Trefousse, "Carl Schurz: Myth and Reality," *Yearbook of German-American Studies.* 19(1984): 1-16. DHT.

5. Regarding the importance of German editions of Filson's history for German image of the region, see Don Heinrich Tolzmann, ed., *Das Ohiotal - The Ohio Valley: The German Dimension*. (New York: Peter Lang Pub. Co., 1993), pp. 22-23. DHT.

6. For further information regarding the importance of German publications for the German immigration, see Tolzmann, *Das Ohiotal*, pp. 21-37. DHT.

7. Tacitus, the Roman historian, wrote of the early Germans and their customs and traditions in his work *The Germania* in 98 A.D. DHT.

8. *Deed Record*. Vol. A, pp. 15, 40, 43, 45, 55, 60, 71, 84, 88-89, 94, 105, 120, 128, 207. The names listed by now have been largely Anglicized to varying degrees. Rank's *History of Lexington* lists, for example, the minister Tischmann as Dishman; the schoolmaster Löhri as Leary; and the others as: Lamkard, Springle, Kiser, Webber, Adams, Haggard, Myers, and Bushart. The name of Howe is of north German origin. HAR.

6. The Blue Grass Region

Now that we have followed the history of the Germans in Kentucky to 1800, especially in Lexington, we can now move on to a survey of the Germans in the surrounding Blue Grass Region.

The Blue Grass Region embraces an area in the northern part of the state, the eastern boundary of which is a line drawn from the Ohio River, opposite Portsmouth, extending southwest to the confluence of the Red River and the Kentucky River. The southern and western boundaries are formed by the Kentucky River, and the northern by the Ohio River. The bluish-green color which the grass shows there, and which the same grass loses when planted elsewhere, has given the region its name.

The whole area is very fertile, with tobacco, wheat, corn, flax, and hemp, being the best products; the horses and cattle of this region are famous. At the actual center of the region is the town of Paris in Bourbon County. Many Germans participated in the first settlement of the region, among them the following pioneers:

In Jessamine County: the Prior's, Mueller's, Poythress's; Franz Poythress was one of the pioneers of German Methodism in Kentucky. He came in 1788 with Heinrich Buerchett, or Birchett, from the German settlements in Virginia. Buerchett later returned to Virginia, while Poythress died in Jessamine County at the country estate of his sister in 1818.

A considerable number of German-American Revolutionary War veterans also settled the Blue Grass Region, especially those from Virginia, as it had established a bounty consisting of a land grant to its soldiers. The land they received, was located in Kentucky and Ohio, and which belonged to Virginia at the time; the district in Ohio, between the Scioto and Miami Rivers is still, hence, referred to as the "Virginia Military Lands."

Therefore, a great number of veterans came from Virginia, among them many Germans, as they could pick and choose their own land. Only few of their names have been preserved. Those that drew government pensions in accordance with the federal laws of 1818, 1828, and 1832, however, have been recorded in the pension report of 1835, and a list of those German-Americans will be provided here for those counties, along with their age in 1835, or the date of their demise.

48

In Jessamine County, there were the following German-American veterans of the American Revolution: Johannes Ficklin, 64 (d. 1819); Michael Gruenstaff, 80; Johann Gilloch, 81; Jakob Richard, 78; Daniel Ross, 79; Wilhelm Scharf, 70 (d. 1822); Samuel Weiss, 78 (d. 1821); Jakob Martin, 75. They were all members of the Continental Army of the Revolution. The following belonged to the militia of the Revolutionary War: Abraham Cassel, 79; Jakob Gruenstaff, 69; Franz Mueller, 86; and Samuel Reiss, 73.

In neighboring Woodford County, numerous Germans from Virginia and North Carolina, began settling down near the year 1788, after the well known Captain Johannes Arnold had established a station there at the small Benson Creek, about seven or eight miles above Frankfort. Arnold's Station was at that time the outermost post against the Indians, and as the Captain did not have enough forces to maintain the station, it was abandoned. The post was then re-established in 1786, and a fort was constructed there, around which the settlers then settled down.

The following families belonged to the first ones there: Moss, Hollmann, Schlachter, Fuchs, Johannes Koch, Hermann Boehmer, Jakob Kaufmann, Wilhelm Schrim (Chrim), Johann Dimint, Hans Lucket, and others. Under the direction of Ludwig Sublette, a Parisian adventurer, who had landed in Kentucky, they established the quaint little town of Versailles (1790), where in the following years the Marquis de Calmes settled down, who may be considered one of the foremost founders of Kentucky's aristocracy of that era. Woodford County, according to Collins, was mainly settled by emigrants from Virginia and West Virginia; However, there were also families from the states of North Carolina, Maryland, Pennsylvania, and New Jersey, as well as a respectable number directly from Ireland and Germany.[1]

German-American veterans of the American Revolution in Woodford County: The Continental troops were: Nikolaus Becker; Thomas Kuhlmann, 68 in 1820; Wilhelm Dell, 64 in 1820; Johannes Dosse, 74 in 1835; Leonhard Moeble, 78 (d. 1829); Jakob Arnold, 79; Marqui Marcus de Calmes, Captain in Lanzun's Corps, 80 (d. 27 February 1834); Johannes Gregor, 76; Robert Hummel, 80; Captain S. P. Minzes, 76; Johann Schmidt, 82. The following were members of the Militia: Edmund Boll, 79; Robert Schwartz, 84; Wilhelm Martin, 85; Wilhelm Schmitty, 85; Rudolph Schmitty, 75; Heinrich Schmidt, 80; Robert Twyman, 75; and Ernst

Wingfield. The following invalid veterans from the War of 1812, who resided in the County in 1835 were: Johann Braun, Edmund Ducker, and Johannes Kersiner.

Of particular importance for the history of Germans in Kentucky is the settlement of Franklin County and the capital city of Frankfort. It is unusual that there are almost no historical references to the history of the numerous German settlements in the West in the 18th and early 19th centuries, whereas there frequently is information on those in the East. In the comprehensive work of Collins, we find the most detailed kind of information about the tiniest nests, but almost no information is available on the areas of Boone, Franklin, and Bourbon, which were heavily settled by Germans.

Hence, the early history of Frankfort, Kentucky, is relatively inaccessible. Even General Wilkinson's memoirs do not mention that he was one of the co-founders of the city, although this is mentioned by Collins, who also mentions, besides Wilkinson, the following as the founders of Frankfort: Daniel Gano and Daniel Weissiger.[2] The city was founded, according to the same source, in 1787.

Only in December 1802, were the landowners entered into the land registry, which by this time had experienced a number of changes. Here we find a great number of English and Irish names among the original German founders of the city. Of the latter, we list only a few: Johannes, Jakob and Samuel Braun (Brown), Christopher Cammack, Jakob Casselmann, Heinrich Gulliam,[3] Pashcal and Thomas Hickmann, Hans Juenger, Nickolaus Lason, Georg Rauling, Johannes Rennick, Adam Saltzmann, Johannes Schmidt, Kaspar Vorhees, Peter Gerhard Vorhees, Johann Wassit, and Daniel Weissiger.

Moreover, we find the following among the first settlers: Dr. Louis Marschall, the first physician in Frankfort and father of the well-known Heinrich Marschall; Jakob Melanchton, who opened the first store in Frankfort and Karl Springer, the father of the magnanimous philanthropist who supported the Music Hall in Cincinnati, Reuben R. Springer, who was born in 1800 in Frankfort. Karl Springer was born of German parents in Botetart County, Virginia on 12 June 1768. As a 20-year old, he came to Fayette County, Kentucky in 1788. After having married there, he then moved to Frankfort, where he served as the postmaster during the terms of presidents Jefferson and Madison and up to the time of his death in 1814.

Springer has also participated in the campaign of General Wayne to the Maumee in 1794.

Of these persons, we only know that the majority of them arrived from Germany under the direction of Daniel Weissiger, in ca. 1786/87, and that most of them were from Frankfort or Hanau. They came, as it was related to me by one of the descendants, first to Norfolk, and from there to Staunton in the Shenandoah Valley. There they were joined by Johannes Braun, whose father was a Reformed minister there. Braun, a veteran of the American Revolution, came to Kentucky in 1782, and during a visit at his home, he suggested that the recently arrived Germans move to Kentucky and settle there, which they all decided to do.

Daniel Weissiger is considered the actual founder of Frankfort, but there is extremely little information available about him. In 1797, he was the owner of a billiard table, possible the first one in Kentucky, which he had to pay duty on. Moreover, he paid taxes on a wagon, of which there were only 6 at that time in Frankfort. Three carriages were in town, a luxury which was indulged in by Governor James Garrard; the Secretary of State, Heinrich Toulmin; and Georg Raulin, who also taxed these vehicles. In this year, a store was maintained in Lang Street by a certain Johann Wassit. Frankfort at that time, according to the census commissioners John Jamison and Heinrich Gulliam, had a population of 441, which included 112 blacks.

It is a difficult question as to whether it was the Germans, or the French who had been there in the previous century, who were responsible for establishing the desire for an enjoyment of the finer things in life, but the authorities definitely indicate that the Germans were there and involved in such pursuits.

The Scottish traveler, John Melish, who visited Frankfort in 1810, reported that a theater was being constructed to provide entertainment for the ladies.[4] To put a reign on the rage of plays, an attempt was made to establish a library, which, however, came to naught.

Revolutionary War veterans: Bernard Clemens, 79; Johannes Krugscheer, 70; Richard Sebree, 82; Johann Hollis, 90 (d. 1826); Johann Lang, 69 (d. 1820). From the War of 1818, there were the following invalids: Wilhelm Guenther, Jakob Jaeger, Thomas Hickman, and Franz L. Schlachter (d. 1832).

Scott County, located to the east of Franklin County, had only a few German settlers, including the Pennsylvania German General Joseph Descha and Jakob Stucker, who had a farm at the North Elkhorn River, and from whom the Indians stole three horses in 1788.

Revolutionary War veterans in Scott County: Nathaniel Muttershaupt, 83; Heinrich Braun, 83 (d. 1830); Karl Erwin, 67 (d. 1820); Thomas Paslay (Paessle), 78; Moritze Halle, 67 (d. 1822); Gerhard Schmidt, 64 in 1820; N. Jung, 108 in 1820; Heinrich Huss, 79; Johann Jacobs (cavalry), 72; David Kehr, 77; Paul Leder (sergeant), 88; Johannes Miller; Adam Schlapp, 79; Johannes Vinzent, 70; Militia: Joseph Burg, 72; Thomas Braun, 89; Johann Garth, 72; Jakob Twymann (d. 1834); Johann Heiles, 72; Hans Sugget, 83; Johannes Schaaf, 71.

With regard to Owens County, there is no information about the German settlers with the exception of the names of the following Revolutionary War soldiers: Line: Lorenz Huber, 84; Jakob Jaeger, 71; Johannes Kugel, 76; Wilhelm Ligon (artillery), 72; Jakob Stampfer, 71; Johannes Sersse, 72. Militia: Wilhelm Lorenz (Lorance), 71; Johann Sanders, 83; Heinrich Thun, 78; Ludwig Vallendinheim and Johannes Wilheut (Wilhite.)

In Grant County, however, we find a rather large number of Germans. Johannes Zinn settled down at Fork Lick Creek in 1792. We find Wilhelm Arnold at Williamstown; and the following at other places in the county: Philipp Gauch; Heinrich Schilder; Jakob Theobald; Karl Sechrist; Wilhelm Layton (?); Karl Daniel; Jakob Neu; Johannes Page; and Philipp Busch.

Johannes Gruenle bought a 200 acre farm for 5 L on 27 September 1796 at the northern fork of Eagle Creek, which he settled down on in the fall of that year. Wilhelm Konrad Wall was the first lawyer in the county, which was organized in 1820. At the Elkhorn River in Grant County there were several Germans in the years 1828-29, who had a store there. This was owned by Jakob Koehne, who died in Cincinnati, and Franz Joseph Arenz, the founder of Arenzville, Illinois. They mainly dealt with drapery and smallwares, and employed several German peddlers, who traveled throughout the Blue Grass Region.

In 1829, they sold their business to one of their former peddlers, Wilhelm Stephan Utterbach, who continued the same for several years. There is a bit of people's justice associated with his name, and this took place in 1841. One day, he was robbed and horribly beaten in a nearby forest. The robbers, Smith Maythe and Lyman Crouch, who were rumored to be friends, were caught and placed in the county jail to await their trial.

On the 10th of July of that year, a large mob of about 350 people gathered at the jail, broke into it, and took the prisoners to the site where Utterbach has been almost beaten to death, and hung them from a tree, under which they were buried. Surprisingly enough, Utterbach recovered from his wounds, but remained deaf thereafter. The two who were hanged were notorious individuals, and it was always felt that they met their true reward.

Revolutionary War Soldiers: Line: Jakob Betz (Virginia Cavalry), 69 (d. 1826); Militia: Wilhelm Arnold; Johann Jump, 86; Jakob Reu, 73; Heinrich Schilder, 70; Jakob Theobald; Johann Zinn, 71. Wilhelm Arnold took part in the War of 1812 and was a Lt. in the Kentucky military at the Battle of New Orleans.

The first bill of sale in the land registry of Gallatin County was that of Johann Pfister, who purchased a building lot in Port William for 5 L in 1799. Also, the first wedding, which took place in this county was that of a German couple: Nikolaus Lautz and Maria Picket. The wedding took place on 18 July 1799. From this it is evident that there were unquestionably many Germans in the area. However, the aforementioned names are the only ones mentioned by Collins.

In later years, however, we find the following names amongst those of the most prominent of the county: Sanders, Strotherr, Weissacker, Landram, etc. Wilhelm Thomassen, a dragoon in Armand's Legion, and David Severn, 74 (d. 1823), a member of Washington's Bodyguard, are the only names of Revolutionary War soldiers in this county which have been preserved.

In neighboring Boone County we also find quite a few Germans. Collins writes that the first white women who came to Kentucky was Mrs. Maria Engels, who had been kidnaped by Shawnee in present day Montgomery County, Virginia, along with her two children, a sister-in-law, Mrs. Draper, and another German woman. After the Indians had been at their camp for a while, which was located where Portsmouth, Ohio is today, several French traders came to their camp to sell their wares in exchange for furs. Mrs. Engels had made a shirt of cotton, which a Frenchman noticed hanging on a pole. He greatly praised the shirt, as well as Mrs. Engels as an Indian squaw to the Indians. In this way, she was able to escape many of the unpleasantries suffered by her sister-in-law.

Later on, they and another older German woman, who had been in Indian captivity for a long time, were taken by a party of Indians to Big Bone Lick where they wanted to make salt. As Mrs. Engels was separated from her children and sister-in-law, she and the older women decided to make their escape. The Indians granted them permission to gather grapes in the woods, so each took a blanket, a knife, and a tomahawk, and left the salt lick one afternoon in the fall of 1756. Before they left, Mrs. Engels exchanged her tomahawk with that of one of the Frenchmen, who had accompanied the Indians, who was sitting on one of the mammoth fossils cracking walnuts. So as to not reveal their plan, they took no extra clothing or food with them. Fortunately, they made it to the Ohio River, wandering along the southern side of the river and headed upstream. On the 5th day, they came close to the camp at the mouth of the Scioto River, where they had been held captive. They found an empty log house, where they stayed the night. In the morning they caught a horse grazing in the area, loaded it with corn, and continued their flight without being discovered, although for several hours they had been in view of the Indian village. Although it was a dry time of the year and the big Sandy River was low, it was still too deep at the mouth of the river to wade across. Therefore, they went halfway across the river until they got to a place where some wood formed a bridge. In going across this, the horse broke through, got stuck, and could not be freed.

The women, therefore, took the corn, or at least as much as they could, and hurried on. In the meantime, they had run out of food long before they reached the Kanawha, so they searched in the woods for grapes, nuts, pawpaws, and roots. This did not seem to satisfy the older women much, however, and in a crazed-like fit, threatened to strike Mrs. Engels, who then fled, and as she could run faster than the other, fortunately got to the Kanawha.

Here she found the same canoe by which she had been brought downstream by the Indians five months earlier. By this time it was filled with leaves and mud, however. With a piece of wood, Mrs. Engels scraped the canoe as clean as she could, and then made her way across the river. On the next morning, the older woman appeared on the other side and pleaded her to fetch her across and promised that all would be peaceful now.

However, Mrs. Engels thought it best that a river remain between the two. Although she was now in the vicinity of her home, her situation was still in doubt, her strength had declined, and her legs had begun to swell due to wading through the cold rivers and streams. Also, the weather was getting colder, and a light snow had fallen.

Finally, after 40 days of endurance, she arrived at the place of a friendly neighbor family, which joyfully took her into their home and cared for her lovingly. After a half week of care and rest, she had recovered so much, that she made her way to home and husband. Help was also sent to the other German woman, who also recovered from her plight in the woods. One of the children of Mrs. Engels died in captivity, and the other, a boy, remained 13 years with the Indians until the father succeeded in locating him, and in paying a ransom for his release. They later on settled in Boone County, where Mrs. Engels died in 1813 at the age of 84. Her descendants belong to the most respected families of Kentucky. In the meantime, it took many years after the story just told until Boone County was actually settled.

With regard to the settlement at Tanner's Station and the region around Florence, readers are referred to the chapter on the that topic. Kenton and Campbell Counties are dealt with in the chapters covering Covington and Newport.

Revolutionary War Soldiers in Boone County: Line: Jakob Brunner, 75; Samuel Stribling, 92; Daniel Gaff, 80; Wilhelm Golding, 75; Georg Fest, 81. Militia: Samuel Rause, 84; Jakob Rause, 76; Wilhelm Schmieder, 79; Johann Schwindle, 82; Jakob Rudeel, 75; Alex. Ross, 72. In Campbell County: Line: Johann Mersse (Armand's Legion), 73; Jakob Mefford, 70; Samuel Yland, 68; Hans Duecker, 75; Nikolaus Lang (Brig. Maj. & Adjunct), 80. Militia: Johannes Huling and Joseph Hubert, sen. 79.

Notes

1. Collins, *History of Kentucky*. Vol. 2, p. 767. HAR

2. *Ibid*, Vol. 2, p. 707. HAR

3. In the land registries of Lexington he is named Heinrich Gullion. His son, Edmund, settled in Lexington in 1796. He had a shoemaker's shop at Mulberry Street. See the land registry of Fayette county, Vol. A, p. 15. HAR

4. John Melish, *Travels in the United States*. Vol. II, p. 182. HAR

5. See the *Land Register of Campbell County*, Vol. A, p. 207. HAR

6. *Der Deutsche Pionier*. 12, pp. 68ff. It might be mentioned that the name given here "Dewees" is written as Ludwig Dewise in a bill of sale for property at Bullitsburg (13 November 1797). See the *Land Register of Campbell County*, Vol. A, p. 220. HAR

7. *Ibid*, Vol. 11, pp. 184, 258, 309 and 352ff. HAR

7. Settlement in The Blue Grass Region

One of the oldest settlers in Pendelton County was the aforementioned Hans Waller, who had a sawmill in the area of present day town of Falmouth at the end of the 18th century. This is referred to in an advertisement in the *Centinel of the North-Western Territory* of Cincinnati as follows: "Lumber and scantling of all kinds are available at the mill, or in Cincinnati as soon as possible. Orders are gratefully accepted and punctually fulfilled. Johannes Wallere, Falmouth, in the fork of the Licking River, 15 December 1794. N.B.: The undersigned will be coming down river with a load of lumber as soon as the water level on the river permits."

Collins indicates that the name Wallere might be derived from Wallace, which, however, is erroneous, as Johann, or Hans Waller lived for several years in Pendleton County and was one of the founders of the town of Falmouth, as is known by means of various public documents in the court proceedings of Campbell County, of which Pendleton County was originally a part of. Waller was one of the trustees of the town founded in 1793.[1] On 30 July 1795, he acquired part ownership with Johann Koch of building lots no. 11, 12, 17, and 18, each of which was close to a quarter acre in size, for the amount of $91.00 in Kentucky currency.[2]

That he later moved to Bourbon County and there ran a tavern has already been mentioned. It appears that he had the characteristics of the old woodsmen: restlessness and wanderlust, together with a speculative spirit, because we find him in 1784 in Millersburg, in Falmouth from 1793 to 1797, with a short time in 1796 in Newport, at the corner of Bellevue and York Streets, where he had a country store in part ownership with Johann Koch.[3] In 1807, he was again in Millersburg.[4] Also, we know that he was born in 1749 at Germanna on the Rappahannock. He served in the War of Independence in the 8th Virginia Regiment under General Muehlenberg, and drew a pension for two years in accordance with the law of 1818, which, however, was withdrawn from him in 1820, as he was considered as not being in financial need, as was required by the law.

There were many Germans among the first settlers of Falmouth, a friendly little town in the forks of the Licking River. In the land registry of 1795-96, we find the following: Gerhardus and Wilhelmus Humme, or Hummel; Heinrich Schantz; Jakob Fischer, Wilhelm Kleck (he purchased building lots no. 16 and 22 with a house on 22 July 1795 for $31.00 in

Kentucky currency.[5] The farm went later to a German Jew, S. Loewengut, who founded the town of Levingood, as he had in the meantime Anglicized his name. He, however, left the area in the 1820s and his further whereabouts are unknown. The town of Levingood is a station on the central railway of Kentucky.

Demossville, which was incorporated as a town in 1860, is located on the Licking River, also a line on the central railway of Kentucky, in the most northeastern part of the county, and derives it name from Peter Demoss, who settled down here in 1796, and was still alive in the year 1835. He was likewise a soldier in the 8th Virginia Continental Regiment of Muehlenberg.

At the same time he came to Kentucky, so also did Simon Luetzel, another member of the same regiment, who settled down in Pendelton County on the banks of the Licking River. He had purchased a 350 acre farm from Wilhelm Farrow; a second farm of 300 acres in Prince William County, Virginia he sold to a Thomas Chapman Luetzel had paid L813, 3 Sh, 1 D for both farms.[6]

It is evident that there were numerous Germans among the first settlers of this county, as one still finds numerous German names in this area. Many descendants of the German pioneers are among the most prominent men of the county. Stephan Drescher served in the state legislature in 1822; Samuel T. Hauser in 1832; Samuel F. Schwab (Swope) in 1837-41, and in 1844-48 in the state senate; and Wilhelm W. Dietrich (Deadrick) in 1871-1873.

Revolutionary War veterans in Pendleton County: Salmon Billau, Peter Demoss, Johann Glaus 75; Jakob Haemmerle (Pennsylvania Line) 75; Johannes Hand (sergeant) 83 (d. 8 March 1833); Michael Kuchendoerfer (Cookendorfer), a piper in Weltner's German regiment of Maryland, 84 in 1835); Wilkhelm Lothheimer 72; Bernard Mann 77, Johannes Reidenhauer (N.C. Line) 77; Adam Schneider (Pennsylvania Line) 70; Hans Wallner 69. Albert Ammermann and Johann H. Fugate served in the Kentucky militia in the war of 1814 and both were the Battle of New Orleans.

What has already been noted earlier with regard to the paucity of historical works dealing with German settlements, can also be said of Bracken County. In Collins' history there are only two pages devoted to it, and they deal only slightly with the population of the county. This county was also heavily settled by Germans and today the majority of the names there reflect this. Hence, we find that two-thirds of all members of the state legislature from this county since the year 1799 have German surnames. These included: Philipp Buckner, Martin Marschall, Johann Fihe, Johann Hunt (Hund), C. Schinn (his father Wilhelm Schinn sold a 60 acre farm on 29 November 1796 to Johannes Gaertner. This piece of land at the waters of Cane Run is located in present day Garrard County, Kentucky.[7] Robert Schmitt (Smith), Johann Heinrich and Thomas Rudd, a descendant is goes under the name R. Routt; Johannes Colglaser, Johann Kolb, Wilhelm C. Marschall, Joseph Schufeld (Schofield); Samuel Kuehn (Keane); Daniel Kuhlmann; Wilhelm W. Best; Wilhelm B. Cruppert; Johann Stroube; Wilhelm A. Peper; Andreas J. Maerkle (Markley); Robert K. Schmidt; Thomas F. and W.T. Marschall.

It is obviously apparent that these names are all of German origin. Moreover, two of the towns in the county bear German names: Germantown with 351 inhabitants, the second largest town in the county; and Berlin with 125 inhabitants, while three other towns, Augusta, the capital, Milford, and Foster (Foerster) are most likely also of German origin.

The county itself bears the name of Matthias Bracken, a German surveyor, who came to Kentucky in 1773 and stayed in the county for a while. Bracken was a surveyor, who laid out the city of Frankfort, Kentucky.[8] He belonged to the party of Captain Thomas Bullitt, who Governor Dunmore had dispatched to Kentucky to survey the land. The party, which included E. Stevens, Isaak Heit, Johann Schmidt (Smith), and Peter Schuhmacher, arrived at the mouth of Limestone Creek on 22 June 1773, where Maysville is located today, and remained there two days, whereupon they divided into two parties and commenced the work of surveying the land.[9] Further information on Bracken is not available. Franz Barthelmess, or Barthelmy was also one of the first settlers of the county, who established the first brewer there.

German-American Revolutionary War veterans in Bracken County: Michael Diehm 94; Andreas Dillmann; Wilhelm Jakob 98; Nikolaus Kaemmer, or Kimmer (d. 1839); Johannes Koenig 73 (later served in the regular army in the 2 Dragoon Regiment and was wounded in Indiana Territory on 18 October 1806, for which reason he received a pension as an invalid)[10]; Georg Maintz 84 (d. 9 November 1833); Philipp Reiss 75, a musician; Rudolph Schwartz 72; Johannes Thomas 74 (Lee's Legion). Philipp Koenig was 1st Lt. of the 17th Infantry Regiment in the War of

1812, and Jakob Raser (d. 24 April 1816), hat served with St. Clair's Army, and was wounded in the Battle at the Miami on 4 November 1791, when St. Clair suffered the horrible defeat.

Of neighboring Robertson County we have no information as to Germans who settled there. On the other hand, Mason County, with the city of Maysville (present day Limestone), the oldest town on the Ohio River below Pittsburgh, offers much more with regard to German-American history. Several parties have already been mentioned earlier, which settled down in Maysville in pioneer times, including: Hans and Eduard Waller, who belong to the oldest settlers of Kentucky and to the founders of Limestone.

Limestone was the oldest landing place in Kentucky, however not the oldest organized municipality in Mason County, but rather the third, and came into being as Maysville. The year of its establishment by the legal authorities of Virginia was 1787. The town consisted of 100 acres of land, which belonged to Johannes May and Simon Canton (Kenton), and was on the lower side of Limestone Creek. It may be said that a German was immortalized by means of this town, as it contained the name of a Johannes May. There were two Germans among the first trustees of the town: Fuchs (Fox) and Mefford.

The first newspaper in Mason County, and the third in Kentucky, was *The Mirror*, published by Hunter and Beaumont in 1793, which appeared in a little town near Maysville by the name of Washington. Wilhelm Hunter (originally Jaeger), was born in 1770 in Brunswick, New Jersey. His parents were Mennonites from the upper Rhine region, and as they were pacifist Christians, they were persecuted as loyalists during the American Revolution, and, therefore, were moved to a transport ship by the British Admiral Sir Richard Howe.

Their ship was captured by a French battleship, and Hunter and his family landed eventually in France. In Strassburg, where his parents later on died, he learned the printing trade.

He moved to Paris, where he worked in a printing company. In 1793, he came to Philadelphia, where he at first published a French newspaper. A year later, he became associated with Matthew Carey, with whom he published an English-language newspaper. In 1795, he moved to Washington, Pennsylvania, where he published *The Telegraph*. He then moved in 1797 to Washington, Kentucky, and established *The Mirror* there, but then moved on to Frankfort, where he published a newspaper, *The Palladium*, and continued this until 1825. For 12 years, he served as state printer until 1825, when he attained a position by means of the influence of Amos Kendall as 4th auditor of the U.S. Treasury, a post which he held until his death in October 1854.

The first settlers of Maysville included: the two brothers Johann and Matthias Rust; Thomas Jung; Clemens Theobald; and A. Overfeld. Overfeld's daughter, Elisabeth, born in Northhampton County, Pennsylvania (1784), married James Ellis, and died on 3 October 1871. She was the eldest of the pioneer of Kentucky still living at the time. She had arrived in Mason County, Kentucky with a 7 month old child, and had resided in Mason County to the ripe old age of 87 years.[11] Her father built a log house in 1787 with a window, which had six window panes each 6x8 inches in size, the first house with glass windows east of the Licking River.[12] A son of Theobald's, Dr. Samuel Theobald, served as a field physician in the war with Tecumseh in 1813.[13]

The first ferry across the Ohio River belonged to Benjamin Sutton (1754), but already in 1797 the court of Mason County permitted Edmund Martin of Maysville to also establish one. From the heirs of the recently deceased Johannes May, he had purchased all the unsold building lots in Maysville and at the same time 800 acres of land, which May owned outside of town. Martin was owner of this ferry until 1829. In 1819, Joseph Konrad Ficklin received the permission to establish a ferry at Maysville as well.

That Germans belonged to the earliest pioneers of the West, is confirmed by the transmission of numerous stories and anecdotes. In most of them, reference is made to the "Dutchman" as an obligatory stereotype, frequently in a serious, and more often than not in a humorous way, but usually always with the customary German accent. Collins in his history writes of one such adventure story relating to the settlement of Maysville, in which a German provides a comical figure at a serious moment. One of the first settlers of Maysville, Captain Ward, had been to Pittsburgh, to obtain market goods and horses, as well was workers.

He had loaded up a flatboat, which had nothing but slight ramparts on both sides of the deck. There were as many horses on board as people. They traveled down river a long time undisturbed by the Indians, as a result of which they became somewhat disconcerted as to the possible dangers along the river.

As they came to close to the shore on the Ohio side of the river, they were suddenly attacked by a group of about 100 Indians, who ran to the shore and showered the flatboat with a firestorm of bullets. Ward and his people did their utmost to move the boat from striking distance, and in the process, Ward's nephew was shot dead. Finally, they succeeded in navigating the boat to the other side of the river, whereupon the Indians, who were without canoes, ceased firing. Ward then checked the flatboat out. The horses were almost completely dead, or wounded, and some had fallen overboard. The crew presented an odd sight, however.

A former captain, who had served with honors in the War of Independence, had lost all his senses. He lay on the deck of the boat, ringing his hand and crying in desperation: "Oh, Lord! Oh, Lord." A German, whose weight was about 300 pounds, was anxiously trying to hide himself behind a small wooden rampart to protect himself, which, however, was impossible due to his size. In spite of all his attempts at concealing himself, part of his posterior succeeded in always protruding over the edge of the protective plank he was trying to hide behind.

This provided a most welcome target for the Indians, so that a firestorm surrounded him. He tried in vain to change his position, but his posterior always protruded forth from behind the rampart and enticed further shots until the German finally lost all his patience, and angrily yelled to the Indians: "Oh now! Quit tat tamned nonsense tere, will you!" From the boat itself not a shot was fired and aside from the nephew of the Captain, no one was harmed, although the German on board had served with honor as the main target for the entire hour of the attack on the boat. The captain from the War of Independence felt sickened by having suddenly panicked for inexplicable reasons. In the meantime, they all arrived at their destination of Maysville.

Revolution War veterans in Mason County: Line: Leonard Baen 76 (Weltner's Maryland German Regiment); Wilhelm Boeckle 78; Richard Boucher 70 (d. 1822); Georg Breyerle 77 (Weltner's Regiment); Johann Briefe 79 (d. 1827); Wilhelm Dueber 78 (Weltner's Regiment); Samuel Dehart 80 (d. 1824); Daniel Hukins 73 (d. 1833) Weltner's Regiment; Abias Hukill, or Hukins 75 (Lee's Legion); Johann Kervechal 71; Johannes Rust 79; Johannes Salomon 80; Georg Schaefer 74; Thomas Jung 83

(Captain in the 8th Virginia Regiment); Militia: Michael David 71; Moses Freighter 79; Peter Harget 79. Invalids: from the War of 1812: Heinrich Greilich, Judas Levy, Wilhelm Nieves, and Bernard Raynes.

Notes

1. Collins, *History of Kentucky*, Vol. II, p. 676. HAR

2. *Land Register of Campbell County*, Vol. A, p. 4. HAR

3. *Ibid.*, p. 59. HAR

4. See *Der Deutsche Pionier*. Vol. 11, pp. 71-72. HAR

5. *Land Register of Campbell County.*, Vol. A, pp. 35-37. HAR

6. *Ibid*, Vol. A, p. 40. HAR

7. *Land Register of Fayette County, Kentucky*, Vol. A, p. 105. HAR

8. Collins contradicts himself regarding Bracken. In vol. 2, p. 93, he refers to him as Wilhelm and say that he was an old pioneer and woodsman, who visited Bracken County in 1773, and later on settled by one of the streams there, and was killed by the Indians. In vol. 2, p. 269, he, however, states that Bracken was a surveyor, who together with Jakob Drennon surveyed the town of Frankfort and prepared its plan, and here he calls him Matthias and then states that Bracken Creek and Bracken County were named for him. HAR

9. *Journal of the McAfee Brothers*, a manuscript in the archives of the state of Kentucky. HAR

10. Regarding him, see *Der Deutsche Pionier*. Vol. 8: 3. HAR

11. *Depositions of A. Overfield*, October 9, 1797, and March 14, 1805, on file in Mason County Court. HAR

12. Collins, *History of Kentucky*, Vol. 2, p. 565. HAR

13. See Butler, *History of Kentucky*, pp. 547-48, for the deposition of Gerhard Wall. HAR

II. Ohio River Valley Centers

8. Newport

Campbell Count was organized in 1794, and originated from Mason and Woodford Counties. It embraced at the time of its organization the present day counties of Campbell, Pendelton, Boone, Kenton, and a part of Grant County. On Barker's map of Kentucky the land east of the Licking River on over to Maysville is marked as Mason County.

The first organization of the County took place by means of a proclamation of Governor Shelby on 1 June 1795, which also appointed the following justices of the peace, who met at the home of John Grant in Wilmington (now Williamstown, the capital of Grant County), in order to initiate the judicial work of the county: John Roberts, John Koch (Cook), Robert Benham, James Little, Thomas Kennedy, Samuel Bryant, and Johannes Busch. Originally, John Craig, Washington Berry, and Chas. Daniels had also been named, but they declined, and in their place Little, Kennedy, and Bryant were appointed. Of the group, Benham, Koch, and Roberts formed the Court of Quarter Sessions, and James Taylor became Court Reporter; Nathan Kelly, Sheriff; and Squire Grant, County Surveyor.

In the first court session it was ordered that Newport, located, at the confluence of the Ohio and Licking Rivers, be fixed as the place for the holding of the county courts.[1] Newport was selected not because it was the largest town in the county, but because it was the best accessible place from all directions in the region, and was particularly so due to its proximity to the Ohio and Licking Rivers.

In general, one of the major tasks they had to deal with was the matter of the construction of streets, i.e. roads through the woods. Therefore, during its first session, the court determined that the following should be commissioned to construct road from Falmouth to the Washington Ferry, in the vicinity of the widow Stephens: John Koch (Cook), Karl Zink (Sink), Georg Hendricks, Georg Marschall (Martial), Johannes Waller, Johannes Sander, and Samuel Bryant. Most of these were Germans, who had settled down in Falmouth.[2]

On 7 September of the same year, Jacob Bergmann (Barrickman), Nathan Kelley and Jacob Milles, were also appointed to build a road from Newport to the widow Perry on the Ohio River. In this manner, the following roads were built in the first five years:

1. From Newport to Tanner's Station. Joseph Schmidt, a German, was also involved in the construction of this road.[3]

2. From Newport to Thomas Lindsey's. Johann Bartel was appointed Overseer of this road in May 1796, and was followed in 1797 by the aforementioned Jakob Bergmann.[4]

3. From Spielmann's (Spillmann's) to John Fowler's salt works at the Bank Lick. The following were appointed as overseers of this project: Franz Spielmann (Spillmann), John Williams, Wilhelm German, and Thomas Johnstone.

4. From Dr. Sellmann's place to Georgetown Street. Dr. Johann Sellmann was one of the first physicians in the area. He was born of German parents in Baltimore, and had studied medicine in Germany. Dr. Sellmann resided for many years in Cincinnati and the region. Dr. Drake testifies to the fact that he was an excellent doctor.

5. From the mouth of the Licking to the Big Bone Lick River. The commissioners for the project were: Joseph Schmidt, Jakob Sadowsky, Adam Glese and James Spencer.

Another matter with which the courts of that time had to deal with was the construction of mill dams located at rivers. The court usually named commissioners, who had to report as to whether the construction of said mills would negatively impact on the neighborhood, or the trade on the river. The first request for such a mill in the county was made by Johann Waller, or Weller. The mill was built in 1796 on the east side of the southern arm of the Licking River, close to the forks of the Licking.[5]

The commissioners responsible for this construction with whom Waller had a concession were two Germans: Jacob Links and Michael Kaucher (Cauger). The second mill, which received a concession from the court, was that of Jacob Grosshang, which was built in the same year across from the mouth of the Fork Lick at the east side of the southern arm of the Licking River. The commissioners granted him for this purpose an acre of public land for the price of 2 shillings and six pence.[6]

A third matter with which the courts of the time had to deal with was the licensing and oversight of taverns. The first tavern (Gasthaus) in Newport was maintained by Heinrich Pickele. He received a concession an 2 November 1795.[7] Another German tavern owner in Campbell County during the 18th century was Nikolaus Egbert.

The tavernkeepers of the time did not have the right, as they do now, to bill their clientele as they wished, but received regular price lists from time to time, which stipulated the prices. Therefore, in the good old days, there was many an argument about the large or small beer glasses, or if one had to pay 10 or 15 Cents for a whiskey, or brandy. Everything went according to fixed prices. The first price list for tavernkeepers in Campbell County was established by the court on 2 November 1795.[8]

In this price list, there is neither beer, nor wine, and our Campbell County pioneers apparently knew nothing of our current mixed drinks, such as smashes, cocktails and cobblers. They probably drank whiskey "straight" at that time. Later, they had made some progress, and as the later price lists of December 1796 and February 1799 indicate. While in 1796, the prices for a meal (with the exception of lunch, which was lowered to 1 sh, 6 d.), night quarters, stall, hay and grain, remained the same, an important change was made to the list of drinks offered.

One notices that French brandy and whiskey have been joined by peach brandy, and in 1799 a whole variety of drinks appear, with which guests could enjoy themselves, including wine and beer. The latter was brewed by Johannes Bartel, who had established the first brewery in Newport in 1798 for thirsty Germans and others as well.

Still another matter with which the courts of the time had to concern themselves with was the branding of livestock. At that time, there were no fences, or hedges, so that livestock was usually common property, other than when one had branded one's own livestock, and had registered this with the court. Therefore, on 8 December 1795 Johannes Busch registered two long notches in the right ear as the brand for his swine and livestock, and Johannes Thresher, sen., registered his as being a notch in the left ear. Other livestock owners clipped the ears of tails of their livestock to indicate their ownership.

Also, the permits for the ferries were determined by the court, as were the prices. Thomas Kennedy, therefore, received the right to maintain a ferry below the Licking across the Ohio River, and Johann Busch received one for a ferry from his land across from North Bend likewise across the Ohio River.[10] The ferry prices were set on 1 February 1796 as follows: 9 d. for a man and a horse; 9 d. per wheel of a vehicle; 9 d. per head of beef cattle; and 2 d. per head of smaller livestock.

Border disputes with regard to land were usually dealt with by means of the commissioners. There were few other kinds of claims, except will and testament matters. By means of them, however, we learn the names of other Germans, who passed away at the time in Campbell County. The first of such names we find was that of David Lietsch, who died on 7 September 1795.[11] In 1798, Heinrich Boden died, and his wife, Emilie Boden, was named as executor.[12]

As we are speaking of cases of death, a sad case should be mentioned, which clearly shows what many immigrants are willing to endure to attain a new home, and what great difficulties and dangers the first settlers had to endure. Indeed, how many pioneer graves had to fill the soil, before there arose such splendid cities, gardens, and fields?

In summer 1797, a German family by the name of Bechtel settled down in Newport. They came from the region of Hanau, where the man himself had studied stone masonry, and which trade he also established in Newport. They had five children, of which the oldest was 16 years old. His whole wealth had been expended to bring his family across the ocean and to bring them West. In fall 1797, the mother became sick, and succumbed to the fever.

In winter, the river was frozen, and the man together with his son, in order to earn more for the family, took on the job of driving cattle to slaughter across the ice of the river to Fort Washington in Cincinnati. The ice, however, was already breaking up, and when a stubborn ox turned around so as to make a jump elsewhere, the ice broke through, leading to father, son, and steer drowning together in the river.

There stood the four small children, of which the oldest was 14, helpless and alone in the world, thousands of miles away from the place, which merely a year ago had been their homeland, and where all their friends and relations had remained. Poor and alone in a land where only few understood their language. However, the American people are as magnanimous as they are hospitable, and already on the next day many of the citizens in town indicated they would provide a home for the children. The 11 year-old boy Johannes Bechtel and his 19 year-old sister Sarah were adopted by a blacksmith named William Anderson. The oldest child, Maria Bechtel, was taken in by John Hunter, and the youngest the five year-old Barbara, was taken in by a German tailor, Johann H. Lesner.

These adoptions were reviewed and approved by the court on 12 February 1798.[13] Lesner the German tailor in Newport, lived at that time on Taylor St., and owned lot no. 32, which he had purchased from the trustees of the city of Newport for $8. The place belongs today to the U.S. Army.[14]

As already noted, the courts were not overwhelmed with claims, and this is demonstrated by the thick record book, which covers the period from 1795 to 1800, and which contains but a few such cases. The judges were, however, only plain and simple people, from the usual ranks of society, which did not judge in accordance with judicial fine points, but rather according to common sense. Heinrich Brascher also belonged to this court in 1795-96 as a judge, and in 1796 the German brewer, tavern keeper, and farmer, Johannes Bartel, also sat on the judge's bench, and was followed in 1799 by Franz Spielmann.

The court sessions were held in Newport in the tavern of Jacob Fowler from 1795 to 14 June 1797, whereupon the court was moved to the tavern of Andreas Lewis. When court again met on 10 Juli at Lewis' home, the citizenry of Newport had constructed a court house out of logs, which was accepted by the court as use as such with the following entry of that date: "The citizens of Newport and surroundings have erected a building in the public square of said city to serve as the courthouse for the county, which offer is herewith acknowledged and confirmed, and it is therefore ordered that this court adjourn and meet in the court house at 12 Noon." Already on 14 December 1796, the legislature of Kentucky named Newport as the county seat of Campbell County.[15]

Campbell County, therefore, had its own county seat, even if it was a primitive one, but the citizens had not dealt with all the necessary possible refinements. No one had thought about the fact, for example, that judges freeze in the winter just like other people. And, as it became very cold in December 1797, and there was no wood in the court house to warm the place up, the court decided on 11 December to move to the home of the smith, William Anderson, to continue its proceedings in warmth.

If the civil legal affairs were only few in number at that time, so then were the small criminal cases which came before the justices of the peace apparently greater in number. Therefore, the court commissioned Washington Berry, Nathan Kilby, James Taylor, Stephan Lyon, on 3 November 1795 to build a jail on public land. The same should be built of stone, 26' x 30', with 3' thick walls and two floors, each level being 9' high. They should collect the funds from the citizens, and for the remaining L350, request support from time to time from the Sheriff.[16]

This jail apparently was not built, probably due to the lack of necessary funds, because on 8 December 1795, the court granted the construction of a jail "from great large tree stumps, 16' long, which should be 8' high, and should be constructed in accordance with as the commissioners saw fit.

Apparently, however, this also came to naught, as on 15 February 1798, the court commissioned Thomas Kennedy, Richard Southgate, and William Reddick to construct a jail built of logs, 16' long and just as wide, and to present all the receipts for the work. If it was ever built, however, the records do not tell. As there are no receipts from the commissioners, it must have remained with bail and pillory, which had been built in February 1798 by Abraham Vastine and Thomas Riddick.

Of the oldest county officials, Washington Berry can be named, who was appointed the first County Treasurer in 1797. Thomas Lindsay was appointed the first Coroner in 1797, and Wilhelm Germann as the first Constable.[18]

On 4 April 1796, the city of Newport was laid out by James Taylor and the property holdings for the city were then registered. Aside from the Germans already mentioned, we find the following Germans as property owners in Newport in 1800:

1. Johann Bartel purchased lots 7, 8, 29 and 30 on 8 December 1795 for L14, 8 Sh.

2. Johannes Koch purchased lot no. 115, located at the corner of Bellevue and York Streets, on 10 May 1796 from Johann Waller for $20.

3. Heinrich Brascher bought lot no. 46 on Taylor Street, on 5 September 1796 for $6. He also acquired lot no. 12 at the corner of Columbia and Esplanade on the same day for L5.

4. Jacob Bergmann acquired lots 119-20 from Robert Benham on 13 February 1797 for $100.

5. Johann Holland of Cincinnati purchased lots 155-56, and 158 from the city of Newport on 6 February 1797 for $80.

6. Jacob Rüssele became the owner on 11 September 1797 of lot no. 18 at the corner of York and Eplanade Streets, for which he paid L12, and on the

same date acquired from Joseph Riddick for L8, 10 Sh. lots 71-71 on Monmouth Street.

7. On 15 January 1798, William Smith and his wife sold Wessel Müller a piece of property consisting of 120 acres for L200, which was located at the banks of the Licking River in the city of Newport. This Müller was a manufacturer of spinning wheel equipment, according to court records, which on 10 Juli 1798 bound over the three year-old orphan, Thomas Häglein, who should serve with Müller until he would come of age, while the latter should raise and teach him "the art and mystery of spinning-wheel-maker."[19]

In conclusion, we have sketched the earliest history of the German pioneers of Newport and Campbell county, Kentucky, up to the 19th century. We can see that Germans were involved in the early beginnings of the city, and were active in all occupations. They were involved in agriculture, as well as in the trades. The first roads and streets were built by them, and the paddling of the mill-wheels at the banks of the Licking River announced that German mechanics had actively been at work in the construction of them. The first brewery was established by a German and German vintners planted the first vineyards in the hills of Campbell County. The spindle and weaving chair of the early pioneer women of the area testified to the craftsmanship of the German tradesman, who had built them, and even in the court house a sense of German justice and judgement held the balance.

Therefore, the sons and daughters of the German Fatherland have helped this land to blossom. May they not be withheld the recognition they so truly deserve!

Notes

1. "Ordered that Newport at the Conflux of the Ohio and Licking Rivers be fixed on as the place for holding Courts of this Country for the future." - *Campbell Count Court Records*. Vol. 1, p. 3. HAR

2. *Ibid*, p. 5. HAR

3. *Ibid*, p. 88. HAR

4. *Ibid*, p. 88. HAR

5. *Ibid*, p. 4. HAR

6. *Ibid*, p. 9. HAR

7. *Ibid*, p. 20. HAR

8. *Ibid*, p. 18. HAR

9. *Ibid*, p. 29. HAR

10. *Ibid*, p. 31. HAR

11. *Ibid*, p. 9. HAR

12. *Ibid*, p. 149. HAR

13. *Ibid*, p. 144-45. HAR

14. *Campbell County Land Register*, Vol. 1, p. 242. HAR

15. *Campbell County Court Records*, Vol. 1, p. 101. HAR

16. *Ibid*, p. 20. HAR

17. *Ibid*, p. 27. HAR

18. *Ibid*, p. 99. HAR

19. *Ibid*, p. 213. HAR

9. Florence

In 1785, about 22 miles below Cincinnati, the family of Johannes Tanner settled down on the left side of the Ohio River. Tanner, a preacher in a German Baptist congregation, which had moved from Virginia to Pennsylvania. What exactly caused them to move west from there is as unknown as is detailed information on Tanner himself. He had two sons, Johann and Eduard, both of whom were kidnaped by Indians in 1790 and 1791. The loss of these sons caused him to moved to New Madrid, Missouri in 1798.[1]

Before Tanner moved to Missouri, however, several other German Baptist families had settled in and around what became known as "Tanner's Station," which today is Bullitsburg. Among the families there were the following: Dewees, Matheus and Schmidt.[2] By means of these early settlers news was sent to the east about the extremely fruitful soil, the magnificent forests, and the beauty of Kentucky. At first, a few settlers then came from Pennsylvania, and they were followed by more from Virginia. This interested others as well to move west, so as to take advantage of the rich land available there.

News of the settlement at Tanner's Station continued spread in the east, especially Pennsylvania and Virginia. The news came to Germanna, Virginia, where Tanner had first been located. In spite of the religious dissension, there continued to be a sense of German togetherness between this settlement in Madison County, Virginia and Lancaster County, Pennsylvania, where the German Baptists had moved to.

The news about Tanner's Station caused a young man in Madison, Virginia, Ludwig Rausch, to make his way to Boone County, Kentucky in 1800. From Lexington, where he arrived after a quite difficult journey, he then had to make his way on his own through the woods for a hundred miles to Boone County, as between Lexington and Tanner's Station there was hardly a trace of a settlement, with the exception of Grant's Station (present day Williamstown). What caused him to move there, is not clear. However, it can be assumed that he was invited to come by the Tanner family, or settlers at the station. In the meantime, Tanner had, however, already moved on to Missouri. His relatives did, nonetheless, remain in the area.

Hence, we see at Tanner's Station the beginnings of a settlement of a Virginia German, who had moved to Pennsylvania, and then come to

Kentucky. He was actually responsible for causing others to come to Kentucky, especially form Virginia.

Rausch found the land to be especially rich. Mighty forests of the most beautiful trees covered the area. He cleared a small stretch of land in the vicinity of present day Florence, planted corn, which he had brought along, and then returned by way of Lexington to Virginia, where he told of the beautiful country in the west.

He then returned in the fall and built a log house at where he had cleared some land and in 1804 returned to Virginia, and returned again with a bride.[3]

That Rausch's experience had made a deep impression on the mother colony in Virginia is quite clear. In spite of the difficulty of the way, a number of people decided in the next year to also make the move to Kentucky. On 8 October 1805, 14 families together with all their possessions left the banks of the Rapidan, traveling in their so-called Conestoga wagons.

This included: Salomon Hoffmann and his wife Elisabeth; Ephrain Tanner and his wife Susanna; Johannes Haus and his wife Emilie (Milly); Friedrich Zimmermann and his wife Rosa; Johannes Rause[4] and his wife Anna (Nancy); Benjamin Ayler (Eiler?); Simeon Tanner; Johannes Biemann; Michael Rausch; Jacob Raush; Friedrich Tanner; Josua Zimmermann; and Jeremias Carpenter (Zimmermann).

No information is available on how many children were involved in the move. The family Bible provided the necessary guide for the Hoffmann family. If Biemann was already married at the time of them moved, is unknown. So much is known to me, that a child of his was born by his wife Rebecca on 28 July 1809.[5]

These Germans took the way to New Market, and from there up the Shenandoah Valley to the Holston River, and then down along this river to the road that Daniel Boone had cut through the woods from North Carolina to Lexington. From Lexington, the followed the road constructed in 1803 along the Indian path to Kennedy's Ferry (present day Covington), which was known as Ridge Route, which was known earlier as Lexington Pike.

They did, however, have it much easier than Rausch, who had made his way here six years earlier. The roads had been cleared and traveled now by thousands of settlers before them. Nevertheless, the trip took seven weeks, and they arrived only on 25 November at the place, which was to become their future home. On the way, they traveled from dawn to dusk every day, camped on the side of the road, continuing the journey then again early the next morning. Hoffmann, who was a smith, and Georg Rause, a wagon-builder, brought all their tools with them, and when necessary, repaired the settlers' wagons, and actually finished their trip with the wagons in better shape than when they had begun the trip.

On the way, they were able to live off the land, as six of the men were excellent marksmen. They found: deer, bear, turkey, etc., all of which could be found in great number at the time in Kentucky and Tennessee, as well as fruits, wonderful papaws, which great everywhere in the woods. There was no bread and Johnny cakes were baked only sparingly, as they wanted to conserve food for the forthcoming winter and for planting in the spring. Hunting was continued as soon as they arrived at their new home, where the woods were filled with game.

Here the forest was almost unpenetrable. The whole area was almost untouched by the axe aside from the farm of Rausch and Burlington, which was about 8 miles away. It served as the county seat, and consisted of about 5-6 log houses, a court house and a prison, both constructed from tree stumps, as well as a dozen farms. The town of Florence did not even exist, and where Covington is today, James Kennedy had established a farm and a fruit garden. Cincinnati, according to Harbaugh, consisted of two brick and two wooden buildings, as well as a number of log houses. There were no steam boats making their way on the Ohio, no train coming through the valleys and across the plains of the land at that time.

This was the country, which the brave German pioneers had chosen as their new homeland. The families, however, soon found shelter in the dwellings of the area until they could construct their own log houses. Hoffmann moved directly to Burlington, while Georg Rause set up a tent as temporary shelter right on the spot where the present day Hoffnungsvolle Kirche stands. They all immediately went to work, and by Christmas 1805, they all had built their own homes, and they now thanked the Lord, who had helped them thus far.

The new settlers came from a settlement on the Rapidan in Virginia, which had been established by those motivated by religious faith. This was not the case with the daughter settlement in the Ohio Valley, which had been brought about by the search for material improvements of life. However, the members of the new colony were the descendants of the pioneers of a religiously based settlement, and clearly held the same faith. Harbaugh wrote: "We as a congregation derive from the honorable congregation located at the Rapidan. We are, therefore, of German stock, and are proud of it. Our forebearers came from the land of Luther, of which we also rejoice. We are also not like the ungrateful son, who denies and scorns his mother."[6]

As soon as they had completed the building of log houses, the settlers decided to hold religious services in their homes, even though they were without a minster. The first such meeting was held at the home of Georg Rause on Epiphany in 1806, at which time they approved a congregational constitution, written by Pastor Carpenter.

This stated that the undersigned residents of Boone County in the State of Kentucky and members of the Evangelical-Lutheran and the Evangelical Reformed churches, joined together for the purposes of worship, and would construct a church, and that one of the members should donate an acre of land for this purpose. This document was signed on 6 January 1806 by the following settlers: Georg Rause, Ephraim Tanner, John Rause, John House, Friederich Zimmermann, Michael Rausch, John Beeman, Jacob Rausch, Daniel Biemann, and Simeon Tanner.

The little congregation consisted of almost all of the settlers from Virginia, with the exception of: Salomon Hoffmann, Benjamin Ayler, Josua Zimmermann, and Fredrich Tanner. They then began holding Sunday services in the following order: After singing the opening hymn, a prayer was said by a member of the congregation, and then the sermon, selected from Schubert's collection of sermons, would be read by Ephraim Tanner. Then there followed another prayer and the service was then closed with a final hymn.[7]

Thus was find ourselves in a primitive time, that in the midst of the virgin forests of the West we hear the German language in prayer and song, where earlier no other song had been sung than a war-cry from the Shawnee, Wyandot, and the Miami tribes, as well as that of the Cherokee and the Creeks with whom they fought on the dark and bloody ground of Kentucky.

In the summer 1807, members of the congregation gathered together to build a church out of logs, 18' square in shape, at the place of Georg Rause, who had provided the land. The old church was a log building in the truest sense of the word, and the doors were made of clapboards and the door consisted of puncheons with the flat side facing upwards. There were no windows and the light came in only through three holes cut in the walls on both sides, as well as through one in the door, which remained opened during the church service.

For 8 years, the congregation met in the little church without having a minister. In the meantime, quite a few settlers had arrived in the area, and a modicum of well-being had been attained by those who settled in Boone County. Several powerful factors contributed to transforming its status as a frontier post of civilization. The federal government had acquired Louisiana, and thereby had eliminated a possible threat in the southwest.

At the same time, it had acquired the possibility of shipping on the Mississippi and its tributaries, as well as a harbor at New Orleans, all of which greatly pleased the inhabitants of the Ohio Valley. Then the Indian threat was eliminated by means of the war with Tecumseh and the victory at Tippecanoe. Kentucky now lived in undisturbed peace as far as the Indians were concerned.

The main factor, however, which so greatly elevated the Ohio Valley was the introduction of steam boats on the western rivers in 1811. Thereby, the distances were so dramatically reduced in relation to the former time periods necessary for travel, that the Ohio Valley almost appeared to be connected to the ocean. Everything was changed. The products of agriculture were now available for acceptable prices, and the necessary house utensils and family needs, clothes like the objects and items for comfort sank down to a nominal basis.

In short, economic well-being spread throughout the West, and whoever owned land, now had it made, as land was now worth 30, 40, and even 50 times the price that it had cost a decade earlier. And, now the settlers really streamed to the area in great numbers.

The German settlement in Boone County also received a strong contingent from Virginia and Pennsylvania, and even a few settlers directly form Germany. Industriousness and frugality did their work, and in a few years the farms of the Germans of Boone County were among the finest in the West. The only thing they lacked was a minister, who could preach the word of God to them in the German language in accordance with the teachings of Luther and the Augsburg Confession. The nearest churches were in Cincinnati, 14 miles by land and 20 by the Ohio River. And they were only English-language churches, and at that Presbyterian, Methodist, Episcopalian, and Baptist. Lutheran or Reformed churches did not exist at the time in Cincinnati.

Only once had the congregation been visited by Pastor Carpenter, who had made the long trip from Virginia to them, in order to officiate at the celebration of the Sacraments.[8]

This was a real fest for the Germans of the area, and they came from near and far, even from Cincinnati, to attend the Hopeful Church in Boone County, so that they could hear a German service.[9]

Now the congregation sought a pastor, and in 1813 they were able to issue a call to Pastor Carpenter to exchange his position at the Hebron Church in Madison County, Virginia with that at the Hopeful Church in Boone County, Kentucky. Wilhelm Carpenter, who now became pastor of the church, and who was without question the first permanent German Lutheran minister in the Ohio Valley below Pittsburgh, Pennsylvania, was born 20 May 1762 in the German colony at the Rapidan, near Madison, Virginia. His father, Wilhelm Zimmermann, had come to Virginia as a small boy in 1720 with a group of Palatines and had then engaged himself in farming. In 1778, his son Wilhelm and another brother entered the Revolutionary war and continued on until the surrender by Lord Cornwallis.

He served in the division of General Peter Muehlenberg, the pastor-soldier, whose bravery on the field was equaled by his piety in camp. From him the young Carpenter acquired the inclination to become a minister. With the approval of his parents, he studied theology and the classics under the direction of the Rev. Christian Streit, the Lutheran minister at Winchester, Virginia, which was heavily settled by Germans. He was an industrious and scholarly pupil and already in 1787 he was ordained a minster by the Pennsylvania Synod .

The German congregation in Madison County, Virginia called Carpenter as its minister, and the Pennsylvania Synod gave its approval. Hence, he was now minster of the Hebron Church, the same church which his grandfather had founded 60 years earlier. A true German, although American-born, Carpenter served this church for 26 years. He also provided for instruction in the classical languages, philology, and logic.

One of his students was the Palatine-born Georg Michael Flohr, a doctor of medicine who had studied in Paris and then served as a physician in Champagne. He came to America in 1793 and devoted himself to a study of theology. Flohr was active for many years in the German settlements along the New River, as well as in the Swiss colony New Bern in Pulaski County, Virginia.[10]

It was a real day of celebration, when "Father Carpenter," as he was generally known, arrived in the German colony in October 1813. During an earlier visit, he had acquired a piece of property, which his son later on resided on. The Germans of the area, on hearing that Carpenter was going to be their minister, had built a log house for him on this land, so that he could move right into it. They had also cleared a considerable amount of land from the woods and planted corn there in the summer, so that he would be supplied with provisions in the summer.[11]

Father Carpenter soon felt at home in the colony and his work bore fruits rich with blessings. Immediately after his arrival, he drew up a lengthy church constitution for the Evangelical-Lutheran congregation, which was accepted on 6 January 1815. It is divided into three chapters of 11, 8, and 6 paragraphs each, which deal with duties and rights of the minister, the church council and the members of the congregation.

This constitution, written in the German language, has remained in force ever since. Only in 1835, was an English-language version prepared, but until 1846 the German edition was read forth. With the acceptance of it, the congregation entered a regulated order of life. Every three years, three members were elected as trustees. The first to be elected in 1815 on 3 King's Day were : Daniel Biemann, Georg Rausch, and Ephraim Tanner.[12]

This church constitution was signed by the members, and it should be noted that all members prior to the writing of this chapter (1871) could, at the very least, write their name. Altogether, there were 177 members of the church who signed.[13]

One of the first official actions undertaken by Pastor Carpenter after his arrival was the establishment of a school. He himself taught the classes, and there still were, at the time of this writing, German school books there, which had been printed in Philadelphia. Later on, when there was a lack of such books, as well as catechisms, Carpenter had some reprinted in Cincinnati in 1821.

On Pentecost 1814, Carpenter celebrated the first communion there with 33 participants and then preached once a month in the log church. On other Sundays, he preached in the area, at the home of the farmers far removed from the church. He created a ministry circuit, which embraced the region from Lexington in the south, to Hamilton, Ohio in the north, Maysville in the east, and Louisville in the west. Every two months, he preached at the Swiss colony of Vevay, Indiana.

The baptismal register of the congregation shows 109 baptisms up to August 1871. The first baptism was that of Alpha Biemann, born 28 July 1809, daughter of Johannes Biemann and his wife Rebecca (Peggy).

As the well-being of the congregation gradually rose, it seemed to Pastor Carpenter that the old log church had become somewhat primitive and uncomfortable. So on 6 January 1823, he raised the question to the little congregation during its annual meeting, which was held due to the cold at the home of Jakob Rausch. When some said they felt that the church was still large enough, and motioned to construct windows to make the place more acceptable, then Pastor Carpenter broke out in tears: "Everyone builds a good home and leave God's house looking like a hut!"

That had the desired effect, and the congregation then decided to build a new church in the course of the summer. This was also a log church, but one constructed from hewn lumber, and the walls were stripped on the inner and outer sides and chinked inside. This new church was 25' x 35', had an elevated stage and a high altar facing the entrance.[14]

It was, indeed, a splendid structure in relation to the older church, and yet it was quite primitive in comparison to the prunkende palaces we see by the thousands in the Ohio Valley today with their gothic, byzantine, and Romanesque architecture, their sky-scraping towers, their painted walls, and their stained glass windows, their carved chancelleries and altars, their wonderfully resounding organs and their far-sounding church bells. For the simple pioneer Pastor Carpenter this church was nevertheless a precious structure, and Salomon's temple in all its splendor certainly did not provide the joy to the Jews, that was conveyed to the simple German congregation by its new church.

The human spirit, however, does not stand still, and hardly had this level of comfort been attained, than longing for a great degree of it brought about the desire for more. Even if the old church did not have any windows, still the pioneers had found it sufficient for their needs. At the annual meeting of 6 January 1827, the membership was asked if the trustees should take on the task of placing a stove in the church to keep it warm in the winter months. The stove was approved, however, it appears there was no great hurry in acquiring one, as according the church records of the annual meeting for 1828, it was noted that mention was again made of the stove and that a collection would be taken for one from the membership some time before the spring.

On 13 February 1833, Father Carpenter passed away at his home in Florence. He was buried at the family site and a stone was erected which indicates that he was the founder of this church located in Boone County, Kentucky. Wilhelm Carpenter was a man of great character and of significant will power. He stuck with great devotion and firmness to any matter he had taken on, and was clearly unshakable. This was particularly so with regard to his Lutheran faith, as well as dedication to the German heritage which was dear to his heart. Moreover, it was clear that he did hold Anglo-Americans in high regard, as they did not seem to stand for anything.

He placed a great value in the youth, often expressing his preference for them, in order to encourage them on. One day he met a young man, who was particularly punctual in church attendance, quite early before the service. Carpenter laid a hand on his head and said with praise: "Benjamin, you are a good boy!" The youth later became one of the major pillars of the church. On the other hand, he detested the lack of church attendance by some of the youth. One day, while preaching at another church, he noticed a number of young men standing and talking at the church entrance. Carpenter stopped and said with a raised voice: "Nothing, but the dogs are outside." This had the desired effect: the shamed young people quickly moved into the church.

He also detested trite disagreements and condemned any dishonorable by one of his parishioners, according to his biographer, Professor M.L. Stoever. He described him as "simple and plain, his manner warm, serious, and manly." There were countless examples of his character. He was also a passionate observer of the weather, and it was his custom, to step to the door of the house as it was time to turn in, and check the conditions of the wind and the clouds.

One evening, he noted that the door of his corn crib was standing open, and when he went to it, he surprised a thief who was filing a sack with corn. As the poor devil found himself caught in the act, he immediately began to empty his sack, but Father Carpenter told him to fill it up again and even helped him onto his horse. The good man then said: "Now go and steal no more in the future." As he did not want to shame the wrong-doer, bu rather improve him, he therefore did not reveal his name, not even to his family.

At his farm, he grew and raised more than he actually needed. The surplus, however, he always sold for a specific price. At the time, he sold corn for 25 cents per bushel, and refused to change the price. He never sold to speculators. Once the price of corn rose to a dollar per bushel.

Nevertheless, Father Carpenter sold the corn to a neighbor in small quantities at the price of 25 cents. A speculator heard about this, and came with his wagon to Carpenter's farm, and made him a good offer, but Carpenter refused to accept it, stating that he would not sell his corn at such a high price.

In Kentucky, Carpenter remained a member of the Pennsylvania Synod, although due to the distance he could not attend the synodical meetings in Pennsylvania. However, in the records of the synod he is often mentioned, and he always remained in correspondence with the leading officials of the synod, such as Dr. Lochmann, Dr. Schaeffer and others. The congregation also sent its annual contributions to the synod.[15]

He was well known for his patriotism, which he had acquired during his service during the American Revolution. He had, therefore, adopted the following characteristic sentence of Franklin as his motto: *Ubi libertas, ibi patria*, which he entered into all of his books. At the same time, he tried to imbue his congregation and his neighbors with his noble concept of freedom. He was particularly concerned with the inviolable sanctity of voting rights.

During an especially hotly contested elected in Kentucky in 1832 between Jackson and Clay, two of his neighbors had made a wager as to whether Carpenter was for Clay of Jackson. When he heard of this, Carpenter gave them a lecture with regard to the demoralizing affects of gambling, especially at election time, and then mounted his horse and rode home, without a word as to whom he would be voting for. Carpenter was with a word a real character, in whom there was not an announce of dishonesty.

After the death of Carpenter, Rev. Jakob Crigler arrived in April 1834 from Berlin, Pennsylvania, where he had served as pastor. He served the congregation until February 1842, when he returned to Berlin, Pennsylvania, where he died on 14 July1747. Crigler (originally most likely Kruegler) was born in Madison County, Virginia and a descendant of German settlers from the Palatinate. He preached mainly in the German language, and when he later was requested to preach in English, he then resigned and moved to Portsmouth, Ohio, where he served as pastor for a year for a German congregation.

From 1842 to August 1851, Rev. Johann Surface of Ridgeville, Butler County, Ohio served the congregation as its minister. As he lived about 50 miles away, he usually came about one per month. From 1851 to 1853, Rev.

David Summers served the congregation until Rev. David Harbaugh was called as its pastor.

Under Crigler's leadership, the congregation's well-being continued to rise. In 1837, he brought about the construction of the present church, which was built of brick (335' wide and 50 ' long), and which could be considered an attractive country church. Under Rev. Surface (actually Suerfass) the language shift to English took place. During Crigler's service most records were maintained in the English language - the first English protocol dates from 6 January 1835, but the German-language church constitution continued to he maintained to 1846, at which time German was still being occasionally preached.[16]

In this year it is recorded, that the English version was read, followed by the German.[17] Under Harbaugh the use of German was discontinued altogether, although until 1857, the church constitution was still read in German along with the English-language version.

For a half century, the German language had been maintained, like a little oasis, in the midst of an English-language environment. That this was, indeed, difficult, was due to the small number of members of the congregation. As long as there was a sizable number of older members who understood German, then its use continued, but as they passed from the scene, their ranks were not filled with those who could speak it. Still today we find the same names of those who founded the congregation: Ayler, Beeman, Carpenter, Crigler, House, Holsklaus, Rausch, Rouse, Surface, Tanner, Utz, and Zimmermann. There are many farming families of means, and they marry among one another, and maintain their community, which we find in the area of Florence, Kentucky.

They mainly come from Virginia with few exception. The first German immigrant, who belonged to the congregation was Gottlieb Schindler. He was a Wuertemberger, and a clock-maker by trade, who had fled military service and come to Baltimore in 1825. From there, he traveled to Cincinnati and from Cincinnati he came to Florence at Christmas time in 1829, selling house clocks. He was, I am informed, a very fine fellow, who gladly shared a glad of wine and was enjoyed by all. He passed away about three years ago at a ripe old age.

The town of Florence really has to thank this German congregation for its existence. It was founded and laid out around 1820 by Wilhelm Wilheut (his descendants write: Wilhoyt), Heinrich Crisler (actually: Kreusler), and

Jakob Kohner (now: Conner), and at first only a "Cross Road." Old Benjamin Reiss gave the little nest the name of "Pole Cat," because there were so many skunks in the woods there. After a certain Dr. Madden, an active politician settled down there around 1825, the town then received the name "Maddentown."

In 1828, Kohner, who had married a Crisler and hence become the major property owner in the area, decided to give it the name of Connersville, but as there was already such a place in Harrison County and the U.S. Post Office would, therefore, not recognize this name, the town was then incorporated in 1830 as "Florence." Presently, the town has about 600 inhabitants, six churches, several schools, a so-called Select School, several shops, a brewery, a steam-powered mahl mill etc. Most of the inhabitants are German, or of German descent, as the signs on the businesses clearly demonstrate, such as: Wagstaff, Schneider, Schwerdtmann, Ochs, etc. The current mayor of Florence is named Jeger, or Yager.

Notes

1. Cist's *Western General Advertiser*, 18 June 1845; *Der Deutsche Pionier*, Vol. 10, p. 381. HAR

2. The names are Anglicized as Matthews and Smith. See Collins, *History of Kentucky*. 2nd ed., p. 55. HAR

3. This information about Ludwig Rausch was obtained from Johannes Hoffmann, one of the descendants of the first settlers, who was born near Florence in 1816. HAR

4. The name was later spelled "Rouse." HAR

5. See the *Kirchenbuch* of the Evangelical-Lutheran Church of the Hopeful Church in Boone County, Kentucky, Ms., p. 45 HAR.

6. Harbaugh, p. 4. HAR

7. *Ibid*, 5. HAR

8. Sprague, *The American Lutheran Pulpit*, 85. HAR

9. Among the communicants who are recorded in the church book, p. 45, as participants of the communion of 1812 are the following from Cincinnati: Martin Baum, Zacharias Ernst, Heinrich Haffer (Hoeffer), and Wilhelm Beinbrecht. HAR

10. Sprague, pp. 121-22. HAR

11. *Ibid*, p. 85; Harbaugh, p. 7. HAR

12. Note that the German-Language constitution remained in force.

13. Rattermann provides the following list of church members: Benjamin Ayler and family; Franciska Aydelotte; Austin Beeman and family; Daniel Bieman and family; Johannes Biemann and family; Anna Barlow and two

daughters; Jeremias Carpenter and family; Jonathan Carpenter and family; Rev. William Carpenter and family; Ellen Craven; Joel Crigler and family; Johann Crigler and family; Ludwig Crigler and family; Jonas Christler and family; David Christler, jun.; Johannes Chrisler and family; Maria Deer; Mrs. and Mrs. Samuel Delpe; Maria F. Dickson; Samuel Floyde and family; Jacob Floyde; Mathias Floyd; James Grubbs; Rev. David Harbaugh and family; Susanna Harrison; Johannes Haus and family; Mr. and Mrs. Josua Haus; Julia Henderson; Elisabeth Hoffmann; Jacob Holsklau, sen and family; Johannes Holsklau and family; Mrs. William Jones and daughter; Georg Rausch and family; Jacob Rausch and family; Johannes Rausch and family; Michael Rausch and family; Wilhelm Rausch and family; Ephraim Rause and family; William Rause, and family; Balthasar Saur; Gottlieg Schindler; Rev. Noah Surface and family; Aaron Tanner and family; Ephraim Tanner and family; Friedrich Tanner and family; Joel Tanner and family; Simeon Tanner and family; Aaron Utz and family; Ephraim Utz and family; Aaron Zimmermann and family; Christopher Zimmermann and family; Friedrich Zimmermann and family; Jacob Zimmermann; Josua Zimmermann, sen.

14. *Kirchenbuch*, p. 156. HAR

15. *Kirchenbuch*, p. 158. "3. A passage from the letter of Dr. Schaeffer, the leading pastor of Philadelphia, was read to the congregation." Protocol of 6 January 1831, *Kirchenbuch*, p. 159. HAR

16. A son of Rev. Surface assured me that his father preached alternately in German and English. In Hamilton, Ohio, however, he only preached in German. HAR

17. *Kirchenbuch*, p. 164. HAR

10. Covington

As the editor has published a book dealing with German immigration and settlement in Covington, *Covington's German Heritage* (Bowie, MD: Heritage Books, Inc., 1998), readers are referred to that work for a history of this northern Kentucky German-American center. Suffice it to say here that Covington, along with nearby Newport and Louisville further on down the Ohio River, became the major centers of German-American settlement by mid-19th century. Located directly across the Ohio River from Cincinnati, clearly one of the major German-American centers in the U.S., Covington and Newport functioned to a great extent as an integral part of the German-American cultural life in the Greater Cincinnati area.

Although German-American institutions, such churches and societies thrived in both of the northern Kentucky towns across from Cincinnati, the German-language press did not, and both towns relied on the German-American newspapers printed and published in Cincinnati. Even to this day, the social, cultural and economic structure of the area is closely intertwined together, and the regional airport, the Northern Kentucky/Cincinnati airport, is located in northern Kentucky.

11. Louisville

As a rapidly rising economic center, Louisville, located at the falls of the Ohio, naturally became one of the most attractive places for Germans settling in Kentucky. While it only had a population of about 5,000 in 1820, by 1832, it had risen to more than 10,000, and by 1848, had surpassed 40,000.

The oldest German congregation was protestant, but a church was built only in 1841, while the Catholics, who formed a congregation in 1837, had built the Boniface Church in 1838. The Germans of Louisville occupied an important place in the trade and commercial ranks already in the 1830s and 1840s, of whom we only can mention: Schrodt and Laval; J.H. Schroeder, of whom it is said, that he is the benefactor of every noble cause, as well as the arts; Johann H. Roepke, rose from the deepest poverty and was president of an insurance company and was honored with some of the highest positions of trust by his fellow citizens; Georg W. Barth, merchant and farmer, who raised a voluntary company in 1861 and with it entered into the 28th Kentucky Regiment.

Advancing to the rank of Major, he led the regiment at the battle of Kennesaw Mountain in Georgia, distinguished himself at Peachtree Creek, where he and his regiment came without orders to the assistance of a beaten brigade, and enabled it to re-group, and then drive back the foe. He also distinguished himself equally towards the end of the war at Franklin and Nashville in the bloody battles against Hood. He was appointed Brevet Col. at the end of the war.[1]

In 1839, Johann Schmidt, son of the former mayor of Bremen (d. 1859) who had been ambassador for the three free cities at the Bundestag until it was dissolved, came to Louisville, after having been educated to become a merchant at the Bremen trade school and at the Komptoir of the Bremen house of Kalten. In Louisville, he and Theodor Schwarz formed a commercial partnership, and opened a tobacco business, which became the foundation of the present day tobacco trade of Louisville. They were responsible for being the first to bring tobacco from Kentucky, Tennessee, Indiana, and Illinois to market in Europe, all of which became so popularly well known in Europe as Kentucky tobacco.

Since they began their business, the tobacco trade of Louisville has increased ten-fold. They likewise were the first to bring pickled beef on to the market in Europe. Both formed the first German bank in Louisville in 1855. In 1844, was appointed the Bavarian consulate, and in time became the consulate for all the German states, with the exception of the Prussian, which was a position held by another widely respected citizen of Louisville, Julius von Borries, who served in this capacity for many years. Schmidt often traveled to England and Germany, partly for business purposes, but also for reasons of health. He died during his trip to Germany on 8 August 1871 after having an operation there.

Schmidt was a genuine son of his efficient and outstanding father, although he had not been trained or educated to become a statesmen like his father, and was also not active in local politics. However, he was a very enterprising and honorable businessman with an always open heart and hand and for strangers he always was making a generous offering. He greatly sympathized with Germany and its greatness and unity, and like many Germans here, contributed generously to the surviving families of German soldiers, as well as to the wounded from Franco-Prussian War.

In 1836, Philipp Tomppert, a man of significant influence, came to Louisville. We find him often as an active participant of public meetings held for various purposes. As he belonged to the Democratic Party, he naturally did not have a chance of getting elected in Louisville, where the Whigs held the upper hand. And after it had been replaced by the rough and violent Know-Nothing Party, Louisville suffered for many years under its yoke, so that no German, regardless of what the party affiliation might be, had any chance of getting elected. After the downfall of the Know-Nothings, Tomppert was one of the first to attain a position of trust, and was often elected mayor, beginning in 1856, at which time Louisville had more than 100,000 inhabitants, which in itself was proof that Tomppert held the highest regard of the citizenry.

As far as the German-American press goes, the first publication was the *Volksbuehne*, edited by Georg Walker, and which first appears in 1841. It was printed in a very insignificant place, and the editor also served as the printer. A visitor of Louisville, who worked at the time with the paper, reported that: "The newspaper was written, set and printed from a philosophical point-of-view. It was democratic in its orientation, but independent in every other way, and did not allow itself to be slavishly regimented in any way. Even the format itself was not a predetermined thing, but conformed to the kind of paper being used, and which was the easiest to get a hold of. The date of publication stood on the masthead, but were seldom maintained."

After a year of publication, this first newspaper sailed by steamboat upriver to Cincinnati. In 1844, Louisville received another German-American newspaper: the *Beobachter am Ohio*, edited by Heinrich Beutel. This appeared twice weekly, but then weekly after several years. In the spring 1846, Dr. Albers, who had arrived from Cincinnati, started a second publication, the *Lokomotive*, which only lasted a few months, as Albers joined a voluntary company, and served in the Mexican War as a sergeant.[2]

Albers later on returned to Cincinnati after the war, and edited the *Demokratisches Tageblatt*, and then came into conflict with another newspaper editor there, Emil Klauprecht.[3] In 1847, Walker, tried his luck again in Louisville with a publication called the *Patriot*, which, however, only lasted a few months.

Another paper, the *Louisville Bote*, was edited by a Mr. Rohrer and his family, as well as printed and delivered. The *Beobachter* continued publication until 1855.

The Germans of Louisville belonged mainly to the Democratic Party. In the presidential election of 1840 they had been mainly on this side of the fence, and remained so in 1844. The problems, which took place in this year in Philadelphia as a result of the nativists, as they raged through the streets causing death and fire, had greatly upset all of the foreign-born, although the violence had been apparently directed against the Irish Catholics. The Democratic Party may have had a number of ignorant, narrow-minded bigots in its ranks, but for the most part, its members had campaigned for the rights of the adopted citizens and against the position of the nativists.

Moreover, at the same time, the Whig Party of Kentucky was influenced by the nativist spirit as well. George D. Prentice, who was as gifted and clever as he was immoral and without character, edited the *Louisville Journal*, one of the most influential Whig papers not only in Kentucky, but in the entire U.S.. He had stoked the fires of hate against the foreign-born by appealing to the lowest passions of the mob by means of satire, and the lowest and most abusive language. He referred to immigrants as beggars, vagrants, scoundrels, and knaves.

It was, therefore, only natural that the adoptive citizens would also became the target of such wrathful attacks. Already before the elections, it came to disagreements, and it resulted in the Germans arming themselves for protection and then defeating and driving off those who attacked them. The publications of the nativists then attacked and accused them of being atheists, who were disturbing the peace, and denounced them as conspirators against the real and true children and rulers of the land. On election day, 4 August 1844, it came to a number of tumultuous events. Several German Democrats were driven away by ruffians stationed at voting places.

The editor of the *Beobachter* on learning of this issued a printed call to the Germans, warning them to arm themselves, and to respond to force in like manner. The *Journal* immediately had this call translated and printed with the vilest commentary, and then distributed throughout the city. A large mob gathered at the press of the *Beobachter*, and demanded to see the editor, who having caught wind of the approaching storm, had escaped to security. Dr. Holland, a gifted speaker, who had played an important role for a time as a Democratic Party speaker and writer in the western states, as well as Philipp Tomppert, who had both succeeded in attracting quite a bit of Whig hostility due to their speech-making during the electoral campaigns, were sought by the raging mob, but they had brought the saving river between them and their pursuers, and waited several days in Indiana until calm again returned. At several voting places, it came, however, to bloody confrontations.

Under the name of the "National Garde" the Germans of Louisville had formed a militia company in 1846. So of the most respected citizens of the city were members. It soon divided into two companies. In 1847, an artillery company was also formed, as well as an infantry company, which took the name "U.S. Union Guard." In 1850, and later, other German-American companies were formed. They took part in the 1846 Mexican War, and formed an infantry regiment, while some joined into the cavalry regiment formed by Kentucky.

Here as elsewhere, German-Americans were most interested in the events in the Fatherland. Immediately after the outbreak of the 1848 Revolution, a number of societies formed to support the revolution, in which, as we are told by L. Stierlin, Dr. Caspari, an important personality in Louisville and was one of the noblest and gracious persons, played an important role.[4] These societies welcomed the refugees with open arms, as they streamed in after the failure of the revolution.

Louisville became for a time, one can say coincidentally, a gathering place for some of the most intelligent, indeed one could even say, most fantastic elements, which the waves of reaction in Europe had thrown upon the American shores. However, the events of these highly interesting time and aspirations do not belong to the time period we are concerned with here, but rather to the 1850s.

The most remarkable event of the year 1848, according to L. Stierlin, was the founding of the German singing society, the Liederkranz, and is that much more noteworthy as it was not founded by the Forty-Eighters, but rather owes its founding to the date of the anniversary of the French Revolution, the mother of all revolutions, which took place on 12 February 1848. It is certainly a beautiful testimony to the inhabitants of Louisville at that time that they founded a society, which aimed to foster and unite its love of the song, with that of the arts and learning. They, however, quickly realized that a society could not aspire to both goals at the same time, and, hence, another society was formed for the latter purposes, the Hermann-Verein, which later became a beneficial society. Also formed in the same year was a Freier Gesellschaftsbund, which also had a choral section.

We might add that in the year 1848 only individual German refugees arrived here, of which several then returned in 1849. Also in 1849, the number of arriving Forty-Eighters was still slight.[5] Only in 1850 and 1851 did their numbers increase of those who sought exile here. They soon made their presence known by means of their publications and public speaking, and their influence, after the first illusions and immature communistic and socialistic phantasies had vanished, proved to be exceptionally fruitful, lively, and salutary.

At the voting place, they really started to have an impact by the mid-1850s throughout the U.S., and the Republican victories, which were hotly contested with the help of the Germans in 1854, 1855, and 1856, depended on the votes of the Germans who had come earlier, and who found it difficult to switch parties from the Democrats, under whose flag they had fought for years, to the Republicans, where they found their former enemies the Whigs, as well as their most detested enemy, the Know-Nothings.

It was much easier for the newly arrived Forty-Eighters to join the young Republican Party, which represented for them the ideas of the time and of progress.

In other cities of Kentucky, like Lexington, Maysville, Paducah, Germans could be found early on, but did not exert the kind of influence on their fellow citizens, as they did in Louisville. Newport and Covington, located directly across from Cincinnati, also had sizable and active German elements, and were really an integral part of this urban area. The rural areas of Kentucky also should not be ignored. In earlier times, Germans from the east had also settled in various parts of Kentucky, but farmers tended to prefer the north, rather than states adjacent to the South.

Notes

1. A useful history and directory of German-American businesses and businessmen can be found in: *Louisville Anzeiger: Jubiläums-Beilage. Zum Eintritt in das 61te Jahr seines Bestehens, 1849-1909.* (Louisville: Tinsley-Mayer Engraving Co., 1909; reprinted.: Louisville: Louisville Breweries Book, 1998). DHT

2. Note that the German-American press up and down the Ohio River and throughout the river valley was closely interrelated, with editors often moving from one town to the other, especially between Cincinnati and Louisville. DHT

3. Klauprecht wrote the first German-American history of the Ohio Valley, as well as a number of literary works. See his: *German Chronicle in the History of the Ohio Valley and its Capital City Cincinnati in Particular.* Translated by Dale V. Lally, Jr. and edited by Don Heinrich Tolzmann. (Bowie, MD: Heritage Books, Inc., 1992), as well as his: *Cincinnati, or The Mysteries of the West: Emil Klauprecht's German-American Nove..* Translated by Steven Rowan and edited by Don Heinrich Tolzmann. (New York: Peter Lang, 1996). DHT

4. Here Koerner makes reference to the following history of the Louisville Germans: Ludwig Stierlin, *Der Staat Kentucky und die Stadt Louisville, mit besonderer Berücksichtigung des deutschen Elements.* (Louisville, 1873). Stierlin apparently drew heavily for his work from Klauprecht's history of the Ohio Valley, but the material specifically dealing with Louisville was based on his research. DHT

5. Regarding the Forty-Eighters, see Justine Davis Randers-Pehrson, *Germans and the Revolution of 1848-1849.* (New York: Peter Lang, 1999), and Don Heinrich Tolzmann, ed., *The German-American Forty-Eighters, 1848-1998.* (Indianapolis: Max Kade German-American Center, Indiana University-Purdue University & Indiana German Heritage Society, 1998). DHT

Index

104

106

111

Other Heritage Books by Don Heinrich Tolzmann:

Amana: William Rufus Perkins' and Barthinius L. Wick's History of the Amana Society, or Community of True Inspiration

Americana Germanica: Paul Ben Baginsky's Bibliography of German Works Relating to America, 1493-1800

Biography of Baron Von Steuben, the Army of the American Revolution and Its Organizer: Rudolf Cronau's Biography of Baron von Steuben

CD: German-American Biographical Index (Midwest Families)

CD: Germans, Volume 2

CD: The German Colonial Era (four volumes)

Cincinnati's German Heritage

Covington's German Heritage

Custer: Frederick Whittaker's Complete Life of General George A. Custer, Major General of Volunteers, Brevet Major General U.S. Army and Lieutenant-Colonel Seventh U.S. Cavalry

Dayton's German Heritage: Karl Karstaedt's Golden Jubilee History of the German Pioneer Society of Dayton, Ohio

Early German-American Newspapers: Daniel Miller's History

German Americans in the Revolution

German Immigration to America: The First Wave

German Pioneer Life and Domestic Customs

German Pioneer Lifestyle

German Pioneers in Early California: Erwin G. Gudde's History

German-American Achievements: 400 Years of Contributions to America

German-Americana: A Bibliography

Germany and America, 1450-1700

Kentucky's German Pioneers: H.A. Rattermann's History

Lives and Exploits of the Daring Frank and Jesse James: Thaddeus Thorndike's Graphic and Realistic Description of Their Many Deeds of Unparalleled Daring in the Robbing of Banks and Railroad Trains

Louisiana's German Heritage: Louis Voss' Introductory History

Maryland's German Heritage: Daniel Wunderlich Nead's History

Memories of the Battle of New Ulm: Personal Accounts of the Sioux Uprising. L. A. Fritsche's History of Brown County, Minnesota (1916)

Michigan's German Heritage: John Andrew Russell's History of the German Influence in the Making of Michigan

Ohio's German Heritage

Outbreak and Massacre by the Dakota Indians in Minnesota in 1862: Marion P. Satterlee's Minute Account of the Outbreak, with Exact Locations, Names of All Victims, Prisoners at Camp Release, Refugees at Fort Ridgely, etc. Complete List of Indians Killed in Battle and Those Hung, and Those Pardoned at Rock Island, Iowa

The German Element in Virginia: Herrmann Schuricht's History

The German Immigrant in America

The Pennsylvania Germans: James Owen Knauss, Jr.'s Social History

The Pennsylvania Germans: Jesse Leonard Rosenberger's Sketch of Their History and Life